Sinners, Saints, and Soldiers

IN CIVIL WAR STAFFORD

Best Wishes
to the Sims Family,
Jane Conner

by Jane Hollenbeck Conner

ISBN 0-9708370-1-1
Parker Publishing, LLC
Stafford, Virginia

Designed by Merritt Hepinstall

Printed by Cardinal Press
Fredericksburg, Virginia

Contents

Acknowledgements iv

General Daniel Sickles; Colorful and Controversial 1

Princess Agnes Salm-Salm; Righteous, Regal, or Relentless? 13

Clara Barton; Angel of the Battlefield 27

Walt Whitman; The Good Gray Poet 55

Dr. Mary Walker; A Woman Doctor who Wore Pants 73

General O.O. Howard; Founder of Howard University 87

Notes 106

Bibliography 113

Illustration Sources 115

Acknowledgements

Volunteering at Chatham enabled me to probe the minds of the wonderful staff historians at the Fredericksburg, Spotsylvania National Military Park Headquarters. Special thanks goes to Eric Mink who provided books and bound papers for my research and to Don Pfanz who generously shared his materials on Clara Barton.

I am grateful to Norman Schools of The Moncure Conway House who aided me by sharing his findings of Sickles' raid and who allowed me to use his image of Conway.

I truly appreciate Traci Hunter Abramson's willingness to share Parker Publishing with me.

Thanks goes to D.P Newton of the White Oak Civil War Museum for always being willing to answer my many questions.

This book could not have been written had it not been for my wonderful husband, Al Conner, and his Civil War knowledge. I am so grateful to him and my sweet daughter, Michelle Porter, for proofreading and editing.

General Daniel Sickles

Colorful and Controversial

*G*eneral Daniel Sickles has been described by his contemporaries and historians alike as a scoundrel, adulterer, murderer, rapscallion, and rogue. Who was this colorful visitor to Stafford and how did he obtain such labels?

Daniel Edgar Sickles was born in New York City on October 20, 1819. Following in his father's footsteps, Sickles became a politician and lawyer. Sickles who was associated with Tammany Hall, the corrupt political machine that ran New York City, became a member of the New York Assembly in 1843. Three years later he was admitted to the bar.

Personal scandals seemed to proliferate after his marriage in 1852 to a sixteen year old girl when he was thirty-three. Both their families were not in favor of the marriage. Teresa Bagioli, daughter of a famous opera star, was extremely talented for a girl her age, as she was fluent in five languages. Many spoke of her as being charming and intelligent. Shortly after the marriage, Sickles was appointed by President Franklin Pierce to become secretary of the U.S. legation in London. Leaving a pregnant Teresa at home, Sickles took a prostitute, Fanny White, to England and had the audacity to present her to Queen Victoria. Cleverly, he introduced the prostitute with the surname of his New York political opponent.

Teresa was sixteen when she married Sickles, who was twice her age.

After Sickles' return to America in 1855, he became a member of the New York Senate. It was during this time he helped establish Central Park, an achievement of which he was most proud. He remained in the Senate for two years until he was elected as a Democratic congressman from New York. The Sickles family, which now included their little daughter Laura, moved to Washington, D.C. so Dan could assume his position on Capitol Hill.

One of the first Washington events Teresa and Dan attended was the 1857 inaugural ball of President James Buchanan. Sickles' biographer, W.A. Swanberg, paints a picture of Dan that evening:

> The new Congressman was a small man of thirty-seven with the alert, energetic compactness of a bull terrier. He wore his hair at collar length, as was the custom among legislators, and his face was clean-shaven except for a full, drooping mustache that trailed from an aggressive nose. There a penetrating quality about his eyes, and under them were faintly visible sacs hinting of many a reckless outing. Faultlessly attired in a dark suit with colorful silk vest and cravat, Mr. Sickles was an arresting figure because he combined good looks with an air of subdued violence.[1]

Dan selected a family home in a prestigious location, facing Lafayette Square near the White House.

After staying at a hotel for a while, the Sickles family decided to move. Dan, who loved to entertain, leased a three story white brick home overlooking Lafayette Square across from the White House. He hired a staff consisting of a butler, cook, chambermaid, coachman, and footman. The entire place was redecorated in baroque style complete with a well-stocked wine and fine-liquor selection in the basement. Two new horses could be found outside the house along with a shiny carriage.

The recently acquired house became the site of frequent dinner parties and gatherings. Virginia Clay of Alabama wrote a description of Teresa at one of their events:

> She was so young and fair, at most not more than twenty-two years of age, and so naïve . . . The girl hostess was even more lovely than usual. Of an Italian type of feature and coloring (she was the daughter of a famous musician, Bagioli of New York) Mrs. Sickles was dressed in a painted muslin gown, filmy and graceful, on which the outlines of the crocus might be traced. A broad sash of brocaded ribbon girdled her slender waist, and in her dark hair were yellow crocus blooms . . . the picture of which she formed the center was so fair and innocent, it fixed itself permanently upon my mind.[2]

Gradually, however, Sickles became busy at the Capitol, and frequently ignored Teresa or left her at home. Teresa liked to attend a dance or "hop" at the Willard Hotel every Thursday night, but though Sickles liked to dance, he usually found himself too busy to accompany her. Therefore, Teresa was escorted to events by various young men, a practice that was approved of by the Washington elite. One of her escorts was Philip Barton Key, son of Francis Scott Key, author of the *Star Spangled Banner*. Key, known as Barton, quickly became her most commonly used escort. Beside the Willard Hotel, the couple could be seen at the U.S. Marine Corps Band concerts that were held every Saturday on the south lawn of the White House.

Key, U.S. Attorney for the District of Columbia, was considered "the handsomest man in all Washington society" and was almost a head taller than Sickles. At first there was little gossip about the couple, as seasoned Washington wives considered Teresa a mere child who would naturally seek fun and companionship at parties, dances, and events of the day. However, a love affair began, with clandestine meetings. Key even purchased a house in a nearby neighborhood where they could meet. Signals with handkerchiefs were frequently used by Key to alert Teresa as to his availability. Once Sickles heard about the affair, he was livid. Even though he had frequent affairs himself, he did not consider this proper conduct for his wife.

One day Sickles looked out the window of his house and noticed Key trying to signal Teresa. Dan walked across the grass on Lafayette Square, opposite the White House, and shot Key repeatedly, despite Barton's pleas of, "Don't murder me!" [3] A White House page, who was walking by, witnessed the shooting and immediately informed President Buchanan. Buchanan, a friend of Sickles, sent the page on an extended trip to North Carolina so he would not have to testify.[4]

HOMICIDE OF P. BARTON KEY BY HON. DANIEL E. SICKLES, AT WASHINGTON, ON SUNDAY, FEBRUARY 27, 1859.

Sickles shot Key several times. Samuel Butterworth, a Tammany cohort, was a witness but was never called to testify. A second witness, a White House aide, also did not testify.

A scandalous trial ensued, receiving nationwide attention. Sickles forced Teresa to write a confession of her affair. Later, the confession was published in newspapers throughout the land, with Sickles being the only person who would have released the confession. Sickles biographer, W.A. Swanburg, concluded that Sickles was a fighter and by placing the confession in publications he gave "proof to the public of the great wrong he had suffered at the hands of Key."[5] The trial was covered by the media and the nation clamored to follow it via newspapers. One of Sickles eight lawyers was personal friend, Edwin M. Stanton, who later became secretary of war in Lincoln's cabinet. Stanton, in charge of the defense, got an acquittal for Sickles. This was the first time that a defendant was acquitted using a plea of "temporary insanity." Stanton was so pleased with the verdict that he did a jig in the courtroom and called for three cheers.

A May 14, 1859, *Harper's Weekly* article reported that the day after the trial's conclusion Sickles was walking with two gentlemen in Lafayette Square by the site of the infamous crime. It was there he confessed, "Of course I intended to kill him. He deserved it."

To the chagrin of many of Dan's friends, he publicly forgave Teresa and took her back. Congress was out of session after the trial, but Sickles returned to finish out his term leaving Teresa and Laura in New York. Upon his return, he was ostracized by most in Congress and sat alone, so he decided not to run for re-election in 1860. (Teresa died just seven years later at the age of 31.)

In March of 1861, with the Civil War about to begin, Democrat Sickles offered his service to Lincoln and was granted permission to raise troops. About four months later, Sickles, who was commissioned a colonel, took command of the 70th New York Infantry. Sickles rose in rank at a rapid rate. Just three months later he became brigadier general of volunteers. He now would lead the "Excelsior" Brigade, also known as the 2nd Brigade of Hooker' Division, Army of the Potomac. He stayed with this brigade through the Peninsula Campaign.

At the start of the war, Sickles became fascinated with Professor Thaddeus Lowe's hot air balloons which were used for reconnaissance. He often went up noting locations of rebel troops. Dressed in his uniform with glittering decorations, his balloon baskets frequently received Confederate cannon fire which always missed the mark.[6]

In the spring of 1862, Southern newspapers reported that Sickles' New York brigade occupied Maryland opposite Stafford. On April 2nd, Sickles and a large force of "one thousand cavalry and 2,000 infantry" left Maryland by steamboat and traveled to Evansport, now called Quantico. On April 4th, they headed south and had a brief skirmish at Aquia Church with "forty

This image of Brigadier General Sickles was taken by the famous photographer Matthew Brady.

Sickles and his men had a skirmish by Aquia Church
with forty Texas scouts.

Texas scouts." That same day they attacked the Stafford Courthouse area. Some newspapers reported Sickles' men ransacked stores, houses and stole silver, money, and clothing. "We have it on pretty good authority that while at Stafford C.H. the enemy destroyed [and] mutilated the records of the county."[7] *The Richmond Daily Enquirer* reported, "It is said that Sickles was drunk, and that among other excesses they dressed themselves in night caps and gowns, taken from private houses and danced through the streets."[8]

Six months later, in September of 1862, Sickles became commander of the 2nd Division, III Army Corps. At the first of the year, in 1863, he was promoted to major general and assumed command of the III Army Corps. It was during this time, Dan returned to Stafford. In the spring, Lincoln visited the Army of the Potomac to review the troops and visit the wounded. The book, *Lincoln in Stafford*, relates the following story with the President and Sickles:

> Although Lincoln had been cheered in the afternoon, he appeared very melancholy that evening. He and his wife attended a gathering at General Sickles' headquarters, Boscobel. Officers and their wives attending the gala noticed the sadness that seemed to overshadow him. Officers felt that Lincoln made an effort to be cheerful, but his smile was forced. His continence put a gloom on the festivities. General Daniel Sickles, known for his flamboyance, decided to remedy the situation and called over Princess Salm-Salm (pronounced Psalm Psalm). She was the attractive American wife of a Prussian prince who was in command of the 8th New York. Sickles suggested that a surprise kiss from each of the ladies at the party would cheer away the president's sadness. The princess at first resisted the plan, but later consented. After persuading the ten or twelve ladies present to kiss him too, the princess walked over to Lincoln who was standing beside the fire. How would she ever be able to reach the tall president? Cleverly she asked him to lean forward so she could whisper something in his ear. Instead of a whisper, she kissed him, much to the joy of the party participants. The other ladies followed suit. Laughter and merriment followed for all, except Mary Lincoln. Later, to ease the situation, Lincoln said to Sickles, "I am told, General, that you are an extremely religious man." After Sickles denied the accusation, Lincoln cleverly said, "I believe that you are not only a great Psalmist, but a Salm-Salmist." [9]

Boscobel was located at the end of today's King Georges Grant, a street in the Boscobel Farms subdivision. The house was where the Lincoln kiss took place.

Just as he had done in Washington D.C., Sickles held extravagant parties for his officers in Stafford. Princess Salm-Salm wrote about one his lavish gatherings in Falmouth in her book, *Ten Years of my Life*:

> Some of these festivals were indeed sumptuous, and I especially remember one given by General Sickles, in a hall improvised from canvas by uniting a dozen or more large hospital tents in a convenient manner. This immense tent was decorated inside and outside with flags, garlands, flowers and Chinese lamps in great profusion, and offered a fairy-like aspect. The supper laid under the tent for about two hundred persons, ladies and gentlemen, could not have been better in Paris, for the famous Delmonico from New York had come himself to super-intend the repast, and brought with him his kitchen aides and batteries, and immense quantities of the choicest provisions and delicacies, together with plate and silver, and whatever was required to make one forget that it was a camp supper. The wines and liquors were in correspondence with the rest, and no less, suppose, the bill to be paid.[10]

Leaving Stafford in late April of 1863, Sickles and his III Army Corps moved toward Chancellorsville. On May 2, during the Chancellorsville campaign, members of Sickles' corps noticed "Stonewall" Jackson on march. Sickles wanted to attack Jackson's column but felt he needed permission from his commanding officer, General Hooker. By the time he received the needed authorization, he went toward the end of Jackson's column and took several hundred prisoners. Jackson, however, launched an attack against the XI Army Corps which forced Sickles to march his men back toward the rebels and caused a bloody battle.

Sickles is shown here in his
Major General's uniform.

An incident at Gettysburg technically ended Sickles' military career. On July 2nd, Sickles, under the orders from Major General George Meade, had his men arrive at Gettysburg to protect the Round Tops. These were two hills which anchored the left flank of the Union forces. Sickles, however, did not like that assignment with his corps occupying the low ground. He tried to get permission from Meade, but got impatient waiting and led his men over the Peach Orchard creating a salient, or a conspicuous bulge of Union troops which Confederate Lieutenant General James Longstreet noticed. This resulted in heavy casualties of Sickles' III Corps in which it was essentially destroyed, as 4,000 were killed. Meade was furious with Sickles for his insubordination, for he wanted Sickles to defend the area, not go into enemy lines. However, Sickles defiance may have saved the Union, as his maneuvers disrupted General Longstreet's planned attack of July 2nd. Some say it forced Meade to shore the gap and occupy the Round Tops. Today, Civil War experts continue to argue Sickles' decision.

During this battle Dan, who was on horseback, had his lower right leg hit by a 12-pound cannon ball. A surgeon later amputated his leg. Reportedly, some witnesses saw him grandiosely chomping on a cigar while being carried on a stretcher. The amputated limb was wrapped in a blanket and given to Sickles. Later, he had it placed in a coffin-shaped box and sent to the Army Medical Museum with a note which read, "With compliments of Major General D.E.S." After this incident, some declared Sickles a hero while others said that his amputation saved him court martial. General Alexander Webb said, "If Sickles had not lost his leg, he would have lost his head."[11] (After the Civil War, Sickles would visit the Army Medical Museum to view his shattered bones which were on display. It was said, that several times, he brought lady friends to inspect the display case.)

Once Sickles was healed from his wound at Gettysburg, he decided to resume his political ambitions. In 1865, he performed various diplomatic duties in South America and became military

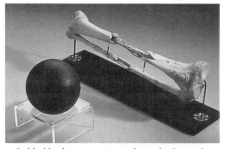

Sickles' leg bones are currently on display at the National Museum of Health and Medicine at Walter Reed Army Medical Center.

governor of the Carolinas. He did not serve the latter assignment for long, as President Andrew Johnson relieved him of his duties as governor. In 1869, Sickles made his resignation from the Army official.

Neither Sickles resignation, nor his amputated leg, prevented him from carrying on an active life. President Grant appointed him as minister to Spain. He served there seven years during which he carried on an affair with deposed Queen Isabella II. This earned him the title of "The Yankee King of Spain." While in Spain he married his second wife, Carmina Creagh, who was daughter of the Spanish Councillor of State. Together they had two children: a son, Stanton, and a daughter, Edna. He returned home without his family, for his wife refused to travel to America.

In 1886, Sickles became Chairman of the New York State Monuments Commission, placing him in charge of erecting Civil War monuments in the state. James Kelly, a well-known sculptor, was asked to meet with Sickles about the monuments. His notes describe Sickles in his late 60s:

> He had what might be called handsome features, and his figure was a relic of what might have been a good one. He had a very bumptious air, and talked in a high falsetto voice with a pursing of the lips, an arching of the eyebrows and a tilting of the chin; with an over-articulation of his words, in an effort vulgarians give when they are trying to make the impression that they are very genteel.[12]

In 1886, twenty-three years after the Battle of Gettysburg, Generals Joseph Carr, Daniel Sickles, and Charles Graham returned to the site where Dan lost his leg.

Later, Kelly talked with General O.O. Howard about Sickles' voice. Howard said, "I can always remember Sickles' voice as he piped up . . . I noticed when I first saw Sickles, I felt he was unnatural."[13]

Sickles was relieved as chairman of the monument commission, for it was said he mismanaged funds. Some said he was embezzling thousands of dollars.

In 1890, when seventy-one, Sickles became sheriff of New York. Three years later, despite his advancing age, Sickles served in Congress from 1893–1895. In 1897, he was awarded the Medal of Honor for his actions at Gettysburg. Some said he had pulled strings to receive the award. The citation stated that Sickles showed "most conspicuous gallantry on the field vigorously contesting the advance of the enemy and continuing to encourage his troops after being himself severely wounded."[14]

The last years of Sickles' life found the general living in a New York house on Fifth Avenue. Mark Twain, who moved to New York, got to know Sickles person-ally. On a visit in 1906, he described Sickles as "a genial old fellow; a handsome and stately military figure." Sickles was seated in a room with many trophies, flags, medals, and animal skins. Twain described the general's room in his own autobiography.

> You couldn't walk across that floor anywhere without stumbling over the hard heads of lions and things . . . it was as if a menagerie had undressed in the place. Then there was a most decided and unpleasant odor, which proceeded from disinfectants and preservatives and things such as you have to sprinkle on skins in to discourage the moths . . . It was a kind of museum, and yet it was not the sort of museum which seemed dignified enough to be the museum of a great soldier – and so famous a soldier.[15]

Also in his autobiography, Twain provided Joseph Hopkins Twichell's opinion of Sickles. Twichell, who had been a Civil War chaplain and Twain's pastor, had witnessed Sickles after his amputation at Gettysburg. He said that when Sickles believed he was dying, he gave a newspaper correspondent what he thought would be his last interview. Sickles "put aside everything connected with a future world in order to go out of this one in becoming style." Twain wrote about a visit that he and Twichell had with Sickles:

> Now when we sat there in the general's presence, listening to his monotonous talk – it was about himself, and is always about himself, and always seems modest and unexasperating, inoffensive – it seemed to me that he was just the kind of man who would risk his salvation in order to do some "last words" in an attractive way . . . And also I will say this: that he never made an ungenerous remark about anybody. He spoke severely of this and that and the other person – officers in the war – but he spoke with dignity and courtesy. There was not

malignity in what said. He merely pronounced what he evidently regarded as just criticisms upon them. I noticed then, what I had noticed once before, four or five months ago, that the general valued his lost leg away above the one that is left. I am perfectly sure that if he had to part with either of them, he would part with the one that he has got.[16]

In 1912, a 93-year-old Sickles, was arrested in the Civil War monument debacle, as it was discovered that $28,000 was missing from the commission funds. Some historians say Sickles' Tammany Hall upbringing and his cunning ways helped him stay out of trouble. Supporters actually chipped in money to refund the empty commission coffers. Again, Sickles escaped jail.

Regardless of where Sickles was located, whether it was at his own home, veterans' reunions, or a funeral, he always tried to be on "center stage." Sculptor James Kelly recalled being at General Alexander Webb's funeral in 1911. Within the Church of the Incarnation:

> I looked for Dan Sickles, but strange to say he did not strut down the middle aisle. But as I reached the door on the left of it, there sat Sickles in a chair braced conspicuously against the door jam with his hat on to protect him from the draft; his nose was shiny and veined like an agate. He was receiving and shaking hands with the mourners as they passed out. It caused a diversion as the poor dead hero's body was in the vestibule on the opposite side and Dan so distracted me that it was only by accident that I saw it. It was the most outrageous piece of impudence I ever saw.[17]

Dan frequently dressed in full regalia when he attended parades, reunions, or funerals.

Several years before Sickles' own passing, his wife, who had been estranged from him in Spain for over a quarter of a century, moved to New York with their son. They were unwilling to live with Sickles as long as his secretary, Miss Eleanora Wilmerding, lived at his home. After Miss Wilmerding's death, according to an article in *The New York Times*, there was reconciliation between Sickles and his family.[18] Sickles died May 3, 1914 at his home. Shortly afterward, fifteen white-haired veterans, out of forty surviving members of the Phil Kearney Grand Army of the Republic Post to which Sickles belonged, held a memorial service at his home. The next day they were honorary pallbearers in a procession from Sickles' home to St. Patrick's Cathedral where a service was held with hundreds in attendance. After the mass, the coffin was placed on the gun caisson, and it started to rain. The aged pallbearers, however, "would not yield to the cold and heavy downpour, and insisted on taking their places in marching order beside the bier."[19] Later, Sickles was buried in Arlington National Cemetery with full military honors. A simple, white government Medal of Honor headstone graces his grave today.

Thousands lined New York's Fifth Avenue to observe Sickles' funeral procession.

Princess Agnes Salm-Salm

Righteous, Regal, or Relentless?

*P*rincess Salm-Salm's early life is a mystery. There are contradictions dealing with everything about her birth and life prior to the Civil War. Authors wrote extensively about this fascinating lady throughout her life, embellishing details, and yet today, genealogists and historians have not been able to clear up the discrepancies. It is clear that she was born Agnes Elizabeth Joy to her parents, William and Julia Willard Joy. One story exists that she was given the middle name Winona by her Indian grandmother in Ohio. Evidently, when young, Agnes had red hair and Winona meant "flame." Other stories say that she had another middle name, Leclercq, given to her as she was a descendant of a French or French-Canadian American colonel. Therefore, her full name might actually have been Agnes Elizabeth Winona Leclercq Joy. She also had an impressive great-grandfather and grandfather on her Joy-side, who fought in the French and Indian and Revolutionary Wars. The place of her birth was either Franklin County, Vermont, or Baltimore, Maryland. The date was December 25th, but the year was 1840, 1842, 1844, 1845, or 1846 depending upon various biographies or stories. (Most likely it was 1844, for that was the year used most often.) While a young girl, Agnes left either Vermont or Maryland and traveled to Philipsburg, Quebec, or Washington, D.C. Another version said she was adopted as a child in Europe by the wife of a Washington cabinet member and was educated in Philadelphia. Her remaining teenage years read like fiction. Supposedly, she was a circus bareback horse rider and rope dancer in Cuba or South America using the name Agnes Leclercq. Others have her using the same name as an actress in New York.

Agnes had a mysterious past. Her autobiography, however, clarified only her Civil War and European exploits.

Suggesting she relished the mysteries, Agnes Salm-Salm did not clear up the confusion of her childhood when she wrote her autobiography, *Ten Years of my Life*. She stated that she would not try "to dispel by plain and dry reality the romantic cloud in which they [novelists and poets] have wrapped my youth." She felt it would be "cruel and ungrateful" to those who made her the "heroine of their most wonderful and fanciful works."[1] Therefore, one has to start the story of her life when she was around sixteen years old.

She begins her biography in 1861 and states that she had returned to America from Cuba where she had lived for several years. At the start of the Civil War she decided to stay with her sister in New York. Her brother-in-law was an officer in the army, so she recalled they "eagerly discussed [the army and the war] in our family." Agnes heard that General McClellan was going to have a great review of the newly-formed cavalry in Washington, D.C., and she was "eager and enthusiastic as the rest and arrived with a numerous company of ladies and gentlemen."[2]

In her biography she gives an interesting picture of Washington at that time:

> The city, notwithstanding some splendid public buildings, most of them still in construction, like the Capitol, resembled a very big village, and Pennsylvania Avenue, the principal street, . . . was still in possession of pigs and cattle, which during the night slept on the sidewalks, even near Lafayette Square, opposite the White House, 'Father Abraham's' residence.[3]

A day after the review, which she thought was "an immense success," Agnes visited the camps around Washington which "was then the fashion." Out near Fairfax and Centreville she visited the camp of the German division under General Blenker.

She wrote that many in his staff were noblemen from well known German families. During this visit, Blenker introduced the ladies to Colonel Prince Felix Salm-Salm. Immediately, Agnes was attracted to the Prince and felt that she "had the same effect on him." She describes his appearance:

> The Prince was then a man of thirty years. He was of middle height, had an elegant figure, dark hair, light moustache, and a very agreeable handsome face, the kind and modest expression of which was highly prepossessing. He had very fine dark eyes, which, however, did seem not to be very good, as he had to use a glass, which he perpetually wore in his right eye, managing it with all the skill of a Prussian officer of the guard . . . In speaking, even to gentlemen, the Prince had always a smiling, pleasant expression, and one could see at once that he was an extremely modest, kind-hearted man.[4]

Many biographers write that the Prince had departed from Europe because of his womanizing, duels, and gambling debts. Agnes was not quite as graphic in her writings but did say that the Prince was "handsomely provided for" and, being very young, he had lived in Vienna in "an extravagant manner which very soon exhausted his means." He traveled to Paris and then, at the outbreak of the Civil War, arrived in America with letters of recommendation from the Crown Prince of Prussia to the Prussian Minister in Washington. He was offered a brigade of cavalry which he declined, as he lacked a command of English. Instead, he wished to serve with his countrymen and, therefore, served under Blenker.

Prince Felix Salm-Salm received his military education in Berlin as a cavalryman. In America, he offered his services to the Federal authorities.

Discretely, Agnes did not tell the details of their romance, but she wrote that they soon saw each other again, and the Prince proposed. The couple married on August 30, 1862, at St. Patrick's Church in Washington, D.C., as the Prince was Catholic.

When Agnes' new husband was in the field, she stayed with her sister in Washington, D.C. where her brother-in-law was now stationed. The newly-weds wrote each other every day, but they did not receive a letter a day due to the irregularity of the mail. Once she recalled receiving sixteen letters in one day. In her letters and writings she always referred to him as Salm rather than Felix or Salm-Salm. Since the Prince was trying to learn to speak the language of America, all the letters were written in English.

While in Washington, Agnes discovered that she would have to help her husband out, for he still had difficulty speaking English. As she wrote, "I soon became aware that we could never progress or succeed much in America without the help of influential friends, and whilst my husband did his duty in the field I tried to win the good opinion and kind interest of men who might be supposed to be able to assist him."[5] One such influential person she met in Washington was New York Senator, Ira Harris, who was known to be a good friend of the Germans. When Agnes heard that Salm would be dismissed by Edwin Stanton, secretary of war, she said "very prompt action was required." She left for New York to meet with Senator Harris in hopes he would take her to meet with New York Governor Edwin Morgan. According to Harris, Morgan had never been influenced by any woman and had the reputation of being a "woman hater." Nevertheless, the governor was evidently impressed when he heard that a princess was eager to see him, and he gave her an audience. Agnes pleaded for her husband, and after a while he actually offered Salm a commission as a colonel commanding a German regiment, the 8th New York Infantry. Senator Harris could not believe Agnes' success. Agnes later delivered the commission document to Salm and recalled, "We both shed tears of joy."

In the fall of 1862, the prince went to join his regiment in West Virginia. Agnes visited him a few times, but returned to Washington and stayed at the National Hotel. [6] In the winter, Salm's troops received orders to go to Stafford. However,

Salm did not participate in the Battle of Fredericksburg, as his XII Corps arrived late. The 8th New York was then camped in a pine grove on the slope of a hill by the Potomac River. The princess went down the river by gunboat. At Aquia Landing, she traveled by ambulance to Salm's camp. She was so pleased to be there and wrote, "It was a beautiful spot, and the weather was extremely mild and fine on December 25, Salm's and my birthday. The sun was shining brightly, and the birds were singing in the grove."[7]

In January of 1863, the 8th New York received orders to march to Aquia Creek. Agnes said the march was very difficult since the "soldiers sunk up to their knees in the mud, and the waggons [sic] and guns were often not to be moved by a whole herd of horses or mules."[8] Thinking that they would probably be there all winter, the prince obtained a large hospital tent that they "decorated very tastefully and even gorgeously; for amongst the soldiers of his regiment were workmen of all trades; upholsters, carpenters &c." She said that the floor was covered with boards and then a carpet. Soldiers made the royal couple a "splendid sofa." Even though the cushions were made of straw, they were covered with damask. Their bedroom looked "splendid" too. The bed frame was large and held a straw mattress. The mattress was covered with blankets and a buffalo robe. Over their heads was an arched "canopy, decorated with white and red damask, and the whole looked quite grand."[9] At the back of their "canvas palace" was a smaller tent used as a kitchen and as a "dormitory" for Agnes' "negro servant girl" whom she brought from Washington and a shed that was used for their horses.

While encamped in Stafford, Felix and Agnes held receptions in their tent.

During the same month that the Salms were encamped by Aquia Creek, General Hooker took over command of the Army of the Potomac from General Burnside. Previously, under Burnside, the army had scant and poor food, mainly field rations of hardtack and salt pork. Hooker immediately tried to improve the conditions of the soldiers by establishing bakeries throughout Stafford and giving men freshly baked bread. He also gave them fresh meat, vegetables, and fish. Princess Agnes wrote that "victuals of all kinds were abundant." She said that they even had a wine cellar, a hole in the ground, which contained various bottles of "different shapes and contents."[10] Initially, Hooker also allowed officers to bring family members to the camps. Agnes said that shanties or blockhouses sprang up beside tents like mushrooms. In the daytime Agnes would visit neighbors, who she said were very "pleasant people." In the evening they had receptions in their tent and would play "rubber of whist" (a card game, an early form of bridge) and drink eggnog or punch. They would usually retire at midnight. Agnes liked life here and wrote, "I felt as happy as could be, and remember still with delight that time."

In April of 1863, President Lincoln came to Stafford to review the troops whom Hooker boldly described as, "the finest Army on the planet."[11] Agnes described the president in great detail:

> People said that his face was ugly . . . but he never appeared ugly to me, for his face, beaming with boundless kindness and benevolence towards mankind, had the stamp of intellectual beauty. I could not look into it without feeling kindly toward him . . . There was in his face, besides kindness and melancholy, a sly humour flickering around the corners of his big mouth and his rather small and somewhat tired-looking eyes . . . He was tall and thin, with enormously long loose arms and big hands, and long legs ending with feet such as I never saw before; one of his shoes might have served Commodore Nutt as a boat. (Nutt was a little person who reviewed troops with Lincoln when he was in Stafford.) He had very large ears standing off a little, and when he was in good humour I always expected him to flap with them like a good-natured elephant.[12]

Agnes, who kissed Lincoln during one of his Stafford visits, remembered him as a "good and just man." (See page 6)

The next year, in 1864, Princess Salm-Salm went to the White House and met with General Ulysses S. Grant who had been appointed General-in-Chief of the Union Army. In her autobiography, she painted a less than positive picture of the man. Perhaps her feelings of him were colored by his negative opinion of foreign officers.

In June of that year, Salm was appointed colonel of the 68th New York Volunteers. But prior to this appointment, the draft was enacted, and, given its unpopularity in New York, it was difficult for Salm to raise 700 volunteers. The princess immediately went into action. She contacted Provost-Marshal-General of the United States, Colonel J. Fry, and persuaded him to give her husband all the men that he had at his disposal. But Salm still needed more men, so this time Agnes contacted the governor of Illinois, Mr. Richard Yates. Here too, she achieved success and acquired the needed troops. But there was one condition, the Princess had to became a captain. She describes this unique happening in her autobiography:

> The Governor promised me a company from Illinois, but said that he would not have it commanded by any 'New York pumpkin,' and proposed that he should make me captain of that company. He kept his word, and I received from him a captain's commission and captain's pay, which, he said, would assist me in defraying the expenses I incurred in assisting the sick and wounded soldiers, in whose treatment I was much interested.[13]

Under Salm, the 68th New York Volunteers were given orders to travel to Bridgeport, Tennessee. The princess wished to see him, so she traveled by railroad to Tennessee via Pittsburgh, Pennsylvania, and Louisville, Kentucky. In her autobiography, she painted interesting word pictures of the cities and her experiences on the railroads.

One of the first things Agnes did upon arrival at Bridgeport was to inspect the condition of the hospital. Finding it in "a very miserable state," she immediately procured warm clothes, blankets, and wholesome food for the patients through the Christian Commission. Agnes did the same thing when she was in Chattanooga, Tennessee. Seeing the hospitals "required a great deal," she worked with the Sanitary Commission to obtain needed supplies.

In January of 1865, while Agnes traveled on a hospital train, she wrote, "They are spacious, airy, and provided with all the comforts of a hospital." She found their beds were "arranged in such a manner that the wounded do not suffer from the movement, by means of springs and elastic bands . . ."[14] Agnes' numerous entries about hospitals, sanitary conditions, and wounded men show her interest in the care provided for soldiers.

In February, Agnes heard that there was a hitch in Salm becoming a general. Upon hearing this report, she decided to travel to Washington to see what she could do. After reaching the capital city, she immediately contacted senators, governors, generals, and even tried to visit Secretary of War Stanton. Her friend from Stafford, General Sickles, wrote a letter to President Lincoln to urge him to promote Salm to general. Sickles compared Salm to other famous foreigners who helped America such as the Marquis de Lafayette and Baron von Steuben.[15] After an anxious wait, Illinois Governor Yates, who had helped Agnes before, handed her the commission of brevet brigadier general for Salm signed by Stanton. She wrote of the experience, "Yes, I felt extremely happy and proud. He [Salm] had given me his name and made me a princess." Now she believed she had helped him become a general and returned the favor.[16]

The assassination of President Lincoln two months later, whom Agnes thought was a "good and just man," affected her greatly. She said the morning after his passing, all homes and businesses in Washington and Georgetown were draped with black. A short time later, Agnes, always wanting to take the opportunity to visit and meet influential people, had an audience with the new president, Andrew Johnson.

Felix sympathized with, and served under Emperor Maximilian of Mexico.

In May of 1865, Agnes joined Salm by traveling south to Dalton, Georgia. She did so, riding on a locomotive's cowcatcher and even took along her black and tan terrier, Jimmy.

At the end of the war, Salm's regiment was mustered-out. Without his Union Army pay, he decided to go to Mexico and offer his services to Emperor Maximilian. (Ironically, many former Confederate officers also served Maximilian.) Being a fellow Austrian, Salm much admired Maximilian. Two years before, in 1863, Maximilian had become Mexico's new French-backed emperor but was not received willingly, since most Mexicans were loyal to President Juarez. Maximilian was in trouble and his wife, Carlotta, went to Europe to ask for help from Napoleon. Her request fell on deaf ears, and she stayed in France while her husband got into deeper trouble in Mexico.

In 1866, Agnes remained in America while Salm proceeded south. Once in Mexico, Maximilian had to be persuaded to accept Salm. But eventually, in July of 1867, he made him colonel of the general staff and chief of the Foreign Legion. A month later, Agnes joined him. Before leaving Washington, she decided to stop in and say goodbye to President Andrew Johnson. Asking him what he thought about the situation in Mexico, the president responded by saying he personally had sympathized with Maximilian; however, he felt that the United States would have to interfere and the Emperor would eventually fall.[17] The president wished her success, and Agnes left and boarded the ship *Manhattan*, along with their dog, Jimmy.

Salm and Agnes had a very trying time in Mexico. Agnes developed diphtheria and while she was recuperating, Salm was captured and imprisoned along with Maximilian and threatened with execution by the Juaristas. When she was feeling better, Agnes became a true heroine, as she braved all elements and attempted to have both men rescued. She even stole a horse and rode along with Jimmy and fruitlessly pleaded for their lives before Mexican officials. When bribing the guards did not work, she even clasped the knees of President Juarez and prayed for mercy for both men. This was partially successful, as Maximilian was executed, but Salm was freed. Before Maximilian's execution, he decorated Agnes with the Grand Cordon of the Order of San Carlos. (In 1873, Mexican artist Manuel Ocaranza created a picture of Agnes appealing to Juarez on her knees. In the Government House in San Luis Potosi, the event was commemorated by placing life-size wax figures of Agnes and Juarez in the same room where the pleading took place.)

After his Mexican adventure, Salm sailed directly back to Westphalia, Germany. After visiting her sister in Washington D.C. and thanking President Andrew Johnson for his assistance, Agnes sailed for Europe. After rendezvousing in Paris, the couple settled into his homeland. There he became a major in the Prussian

On January 11, 1868, the prince introduced his homeland, Westphalia, Germany, to his princess.

Guards during the Franco-Prussian War, Germany's fight with France. Agnes studied nursing and surgery at the University of Bonn. During a time when she was a hospital assistant, she received another captain's commission from General Steinmets. However, Agnes became a widow in 1870, as Salm was killed during the Battle of Gravelotte. Not wanting his body to be buried in the battlefield, Agnes escorted and retrieved his body so a Catholic burial could be held.

The same year as Salm's death, Agnes remained in Germany and cared for the wounded. *The New York Times* ran an article on September 1, 1870, written by journalist and Franco-Prussian War correspondent, Otto von Corvin-Wierzbitzki. His surprise meeting with her in Germany helps one see that Agnes was truly a devoted caregiver:

When I was busily occupied with other things I saw through the window the arrival of a number of Army surgeons and Knights of St. John. On a pony was also the Princess Agnes Salm-Salm, dressed in a gray riding-dress, the white badge with the red cross on her arm. She accompanies the celebrated Dr. Busch, of Bonn. I went out to greet her, though I looked more like a robber than a decent man; and several Knights and other strangers seemed astonished that I made my way through them. But they were still more astonished when the Princess, on seeing me, rushed into my arms and kissed me upon my mouth, presenting me to them as her old, dear friend. I knew her before she was married and was the only witness at her marriage. She is a splendid, energetic woman, and the manner in which she has behaved since she was in Europe is much admired by every one. The old King William and the Queen think very much of her, and never omit an opportunity to show it.

Agnes was an active battlefield nurse during the Franco-Prussian War.

Agnes obtained permission to accompany General von Steinmetz and his staff on horseback. Experienced from her time in America during the Civil War, she carried on relief work in field hospitals and camps. She was thanked personally by Generals von Goeben and Fransecky for her devotion to injured men. Known then as "The Empress," Agnes later received the Prussian Medal of Honor. She was recommended for the Order of the Iron Cross, but did not receive the medal, for it was only reserved for men. More appreciation for her nursing efforts was given by Empress Augusta. Agnes was presented with an onyx brooch.

Constantly, in her autobiography, Agnes compared the Union Army and its medical care, with that of Europe. She felt American care was vastly superior to that overseas. She wrote that in America ladies were not permitted to attend the wounded on the field, but only to do so when they were in hospitals. Women, regardless of social standing, wore the "same simple dress, resembling very much that of the Sisters of Charity."[18] She felt this was important, for soldiers might not ask for help if a nurse was above him in social order.

Agnes also compared caring for the dead in America and Europe. She wrote, "What revolted me frequently in the French war was the manner in which the dead were treated on the battle-fields . . . [they] were treated as unceremoniously as cattle."[19] She explained that in America the "soldiers who shed their blood for their country" were "treated with respect and love."

For a short time, Agnes thought that she would enter a convent. After consulting with Pope Pius IX in Rome, she decided against that decision and settled down to living in Germany, first in Bonn and later in Karlsruhe. In 1875, while in Stuttgart, she published her autobiography, *Zehn Jahre aus Meinem Leben*. Tales of her exciting experiences were so well received that a year later it was published in London under the title of *Ten Years of My Life*. A year after that it was published in America. *The New York Times* ran a review of the book on April 2, 1877 and stated it was "gossipy, superficial, and decidedly amusing performance." Despite the negative comments, Agnes' book still sold well in the United States.

Princess Salm-Salm spent the last forty-four years of her life in Europe.

In 1876, Agnes married Charles Heneage, the secretary of the British legation at Berlin, Germany. The news of her marriage to this royal British diplomat was announced in *The New York Times* and was simply stated, "The Princess Salm-Salm has married, in Stuttgardt, Mr. Charles Heneage, a Lincolnshire gentleman."[20] The marriage was short-lived and was later dissolved.

In 1899, Agnes visited America. The New York Times headline of May 5th heralded her arrival stating, "THE PRINCESS SALM-SALM HERE." She arrived aboard the *Kaiser Wilhelm der Grosse* and was met at the pier by her brother-in-law, Colonel Edmund Johnson, another colonel, a general, and a cousin. The article provided a wonderful description of Agnes in her mid-fifties. "The Princess is slender, of medium height, and her hair is more auburn than gray. She has a bright, pleasant face, with sparkling eyes." Evidently, reporters were there to greet her as well as question her. The article also goes on to clarify details of her adventurous life:

> The Princess when approached at first said laughingly that she had returned to die in the land of her birth, but she added that she was really here simply on a visit to old friends. She talked without any disposition to be reticent, and regarding some old newspaper stories of a historical character, said that it was untrue that she and her husband had been compelled to leave Mexico, that it was untrue that she ever thought of going on the stage, that it was untrue that she had fallen from a tight rope in Chicago, and that it was untrue that she had once ridden down Pennsylvania Avenue, Washington, in the uniform of a captain. Having good naturedly consented to answer questions bearing on all these subjects, put by one of the newspaper men, the Princess got into a carriage and was brought over to the Waldorf-Astoria, where she spent the night.

Later during this May visit, Agnes also cleared up the "circus riding" tale when she told an Iowa reporter, "There was that dreadful story about my being a circus rider, not that it has annoyed me a particle. I never cared. If it had been true I would have said 'Why, yes I was once in a circus,' but it isn't." She said that the circus participation annoyed her relatives and she confessed, ". . . it is for them that I wish it righted."[21] Agnes continued to clarify the tale by stating that a *New York Herald* reporter in Mexico noticed her horsemanship and wrote that since she possessed such remarkable skills she must have been raised with a circus.

About a week later, on May 14th, Agnes went to the Odd Fellows' Hall in New York to attend a gathering of twenty-one veterans of the Eighth Regiment, of which Salm had been colonel. (The regiment had begun with 1,040 men but when it mustered-out, only 168 remained.) At three in the afternoon, the princess entered the hall which had been decorated with stars and stripes. She entered the hall to cheers while a band played popular Civil War melodies. Seated close to the stage, Agnes wore a gown of black silk with a long train. Upon her head was a small hat fringed with pink roses. According to a *New York Times* article, "There was a red ribbon over her shoulder, and on her breast were medals of gold which had been presented to her for bravery on the field of battle." Flowers were presented by a small girl, whom she kissed. Then each veteran came and shook Agnes' hand. Afterwards, Agnes presented the regimental flag, which she had brought from Europe, to the group and read the following from a small piece of paper.

> This flag came into my possession from my husband, who was one of your comrades. It has been a pleasant duty for me to cherish it for nearly thirty-five years, and now I present it to you, in memory of my husband. I want you to rally round it once again and keep it with you until the last comrade shall have passed away. Then this flag must be handed over to the State of New York, to remain in the care of the state forever. This is my only request.

At 6:30 p.m. the guests sat down for a banquet at an "elaborately decorated horseshoe shaped table." The evening ended with toasts to "Our Dead Heroes" and "Our Adopted Fatherland, the Land of the Free and the Home of the Brave." Agnes toasted the President of the United States while General Stahel toasted the health and prosperity of Princess Salm-Salm, whom he called the "Mother of the Regiment."[22]

Later, she returned the flag of the 68th New York Infantry regiment which her husband had also commanded. During her stay she was made an honorary member of the Blenker Veteran Association and an honorary member of the New York Chapter of the Daughters of the American Revolution (DAR).

There were two more receptions in Agnes' honor on June 5th. One more was in New York City and the other in Newark, New Jersey. The next day she boarded a steamer for Europe. After a nineteen day journey Agnes cabled from South Hampton, England and announced that she had a very pleasant voyage.[23]

In 1900, Agnes returned to America but this time with less fanfare. In March, she spent several weeks in Chicago requesting funds for an ambulance corps for the South African Boers and the Boer War wounded. Later she went to New York City and attended a meeting held by Boer sympathizers.[24]

Agnes visited America in 1899 and 1900.

Upon her return to Europe, the princess lived a quiet life in southern Germany in the town of Karlsruhe located on the Rhine River. While there she received guests such as Clara Barton, founder of the American Red Cross. As a matter of fact, in July of 1902, Clara wrote her nephew that she visited Agnes in her mountain home. Clara spent two weeks in Karlsruhe dividing her time between Agnes and Grand Duchess Luisa. Clara Barton and Agnes corresponded between 1900 and 1903.[25] We do not know where they first met, whether it was during the Franco-Prussian War or when Agnes visited America in 1900. Their letters to one another are addressed, "Dear Sister," so it appears they were very close to one another realizing that they shared a common bond of caring for those in need.

On December 21, 1912, Agnes passed away alone in her home with no one except an elderly maid servant. She is buried in Bonn, Germany.

After her death, Agnes was not forgotten. Thirteen years after her passing, in 1925, Franz Werfel included Agnes in his play *Juarez and Maximilian*.[26] As late as 2002, David Coffey wrote a biography about her entitled *Soldier Princess*.

This enigmatic woman fascinated people throughout her life and thereafter. As Coffey wrote, she met or knew "four emperors, three presidents, one future president, and a host of other important figures."[27] She was known throughout the world for her daring exploits as well as her caring for soldiers in major conflicts at home and abroad.

Clara Barton

Angel of the Battlefield

Clara Barton was born in 1821 on Christmas Day, coincidentally the same day as Prince and Princess Salm-Salm. Her given-name was Clarissa Harlowe, the name of a heroine from a popular 1748 novel.[1] She never went by the name of Clarissa and was called Clara at a very early age. When older, most of her papers were signed "Clara H. Barton."

Clara was the youngest of five children, having two sisters and two brothers. Sally, the next youngest, was almost eleven at Clara's birth. With more than a decade between them, Clara said she felt as if she had six mothers and fathers. Her brothers and sisters were her teachers and protectors but not her playmates.

When she was three years of age, Clara went to school. Previously, she was home-educated by her siblings at their parents' Oxford, Massachusetts, farm. Her father was a horse breeder and farmer while her mother managed the household. When Clara was eight, she was sent away to boarding school. She was very lonely there and often failed to eat.

Her time on the farm and her experiences in boarding school combined to create a very shy little girl. She later wrote of her childhood, "I was what is known as a bashful child, timid in the presence of other persons . . ."[2] She was also a fearful little girl and recalled having "a mortal fear" of a huge old ram on her farm as well as other animals. As an adult, she wrote people frequently saw her being devoid of fear and very courageous, but "in the earlier years of my life I remember nothing but fear."[3] One day at boarding school she pronounced a word with a silent "p" incorrectly and recalled that older students laughed at her. After the Civil War she said, "To this day, I would rather stand behind the lines of artillery at Antietam, or cross the pontoon bridge under fire at Fredericksburg, than to be expected to preside at a public meeting."[4]

Another experience of her childhood also affected her throughout her life. She observed the killing of an ox with a large axe. After that incident she "lost all desire for meat" and wrote, ". . . all through life, to the present, have only eaten it when I must for the sake of appearance, or as circumstances seemed to make it the more proper thing to do. The bountiful ground has always yielded enough for all my needs and wants."[5]

Clara's boarding school experience did not last too long, and she returned to the farm and was again taught by her sisters. The family moved to a new home where her mother taught her how to cook. She said this instruction was invaluable on and off the battlefield. She especially liked to prepare pies with "crinkly around the edges, with marks of fingerprints," so a soldier would be reminded of home.[6]

David, Clara's brother, became her first patient when she was only eleven years of age. During a barn raising, David climbed to the high ridge-pole. The board broke and he fell to the ground and remained an invalid for two years. During this time, Clara faithfully nursed him back to health. Clara's cousin, William, later wrote of her nursing, "In his nervous condition he clung to her, and she acquired something of that skill in the care of the sick which remained with her through life."[7]

When Clara was twelve, it was noticed she was not growing any more. With quite large heels she measured five feet three inches. In later years, she measured exactly five feet tall in her stocking feet.

As a teenager, Clara had an experience which changed her life. A Mr. L.W. Fowler was living at the Bartons' home. Mr. Fowler and his brother were phrenologists. By studying the shape and bumps on one's head, they claimed to be able to discover what vocation would be appropriate for a person. Clara, at age fifteen, was told that she should be a schoolteacher. She thought this was a strange occupation for such a shy individual.

She read the Fowler brothers' booklets and was fascinated to read that people should consider their own mental possibilities and realize all the potential that was within them. "Know thyself" became her motto. She realized her inner strength. Clara later wrote, "'know thyself' has taught me in any great crisis to put myself under my own feet; bury enmity, cast ambition to the winds, ignore complaint, despise retaliation, and stand erect in the consciousness of those higher qualities that made for the good of human kind, even though we may not clearly see the way."[8]

Clara attended church every Sunday. Her parents built a meeting-house and were founders of the first Universalist Church in America; however, they still held on to the austerity of their Puritan background.

Following the Fowler brothers' advice, Clara embarked on a teaching career in the district where her married sister lived. The little school had forty pupils, and she was known for her many successes. She continued

This is the earliest known photo of Clara. She was about twenty-nine years of age.

teaching around Oxford, Massachusetts, and later moved to Bordentown, New Jersey, where she established a public school of her own. She later wrote of her teaching experiences:

> Little children grew to be large, and mainly "well behaved." Boys grew to manhood, and continued faithfully in their work, or went out and entered into business, seeking other vocations. A few girls became teachers, but more continued at their looms or set up housekeeping for themselves, but whatever sphere opened to them, they were mine, second only to the claims and interests of the real mother.[9]

Fannie Childs, a fellow teacher at Bordentown, wrote that Clara had a few challenges when teaching but was usually able to laugh and shrug them off. "Clara had an unfailing sense of humor. She said to me once that of all the qualities she possessed, that for which she felt most thankful was her sense of humor. She said it helped her over many hard places."[10]

After teaching for twenty years, Clara became exhausted and her voice failed her completely. To recuperate, she left the schoolroom and moved to Washington, D.C. In her thirties, she obtained a position as a clerk in the United States Patent Office. Her salary was $1400 a year. Some historians write that this was the first time that a woman received equal work and wages of a man in a similar position. Colonel Alexander De Witt, a representative of Congress from her home district, helped her get an appointment from President Pierce. During her work there, she was not treated well by the men in the department. She remarked that some loafed and even blew smoke in her face. After a while, President Buchanan was elected and it seemed like she was unmolested. But her friend, Colonel DeWitt, lost his election. She wrote to her sister-in-law that she was sorry that the colonel was going home and would not return to Washington. "I am sorry for myself, that I shall have no good friend left to whom I can run with all my annoyances, and find always a sympathizer and benefactor . . . I am sorry, and if crying would do any good I would cry a week . . ."[11]

Clara remained at the Patent Office and was in the district when Lincoln was elected and inaugurated. She heard the inauguration address of this new Republican president and apparently was pleased with its contents. Clara's father was an "old–time Jackson Democrat," and the administration under which she was appointed was Democratic. She did not know what to expect, but she did realize that "war was in the air."

Lincoln issued a call for volunteers on April 15, 1861. Four Regiments from Massachusetts immediately left and marched through Baltimore on their way to the district. Three men were killed by a mob of Southern sympathizers and thirty were injured. Fighting their way to a station, they gained possession of a train and hurried to Washington D.C. By this time Union tents had sprung up throughout the capital city. Since there appeared to be no room, the Massachusetts men were quartered in the Senate Chambers of the nation's Capitol. Hearing about their arrival, Clara immediately went to see if she was needed. She found some of "her boys" and friends there. It was here where Clara actually started her humanitarian activities. She wrote a friend on August 25th of the soldiers' situation:

> ...their baggage was all seized and they have nothing but their heavy woolen clothes – not a cotton shirt – and many of them not even a pocket handkerchief. We, of course, emptied our pockets and came home to tear up old sheets for towels and handkerchiefs, and have filled a large box with all manner of serving utensils, thread, needles, thimbles, scissors, pins, buttons, strings, salves, tallow, etc., have filled the largest market basket in the house and it will go to them in the next hour.[12]

The Massachusetts men left the Capitol laden with items supplied by Clara. Two months later, in July, Union forces marched gallantly off to Bull Run, Virginia. Clara wrote to her father that the "noble, gallant, handsome fellows" left the district and were "armed to the teeth . . ." Later, Clara was shocked when she heard the news that 481 men were killed, 1011 were wounded, and 1460 were missing.

The wounded men from Bull Run arrived in the district and were placed in hospitals. Immediately, Clara went to see if she could help. She found a need for bandages and thought fruits and jellies from Northern farms would comfort the soldiers. She went into action and began advertising in the Massachusetts newspaper, *The Worcester Spy*, asking for good clean cloth that could be made into bandages and provisions for the soldiers. The response was overwhelming and she rented a large room in the business block of D.C and established a distributing agency. She had a wooden partition placed in the middle, so she could live on one side and store the incoming goods on the other.

A half year later, in December of 1861, Worcester women asked Clara if there was any need for them to send any more supplies. Clara's letter to the Ladies' Relief Committee of Worcester encouraged the women to send more, but she also described the horrifying conditions of the soldiers. She mentioned lack of blankets or covers, starvation, medical treatment amidst decaying body parts, and bleeding after amputation. She said other states in the nation "lack somewhat the active, industrious, intelligent organizations at home which are so characteristic of our New England circles."[13] She continued writing, ". . . our army cannot afford that our ladies lay down their needles and fold their hands; if their contributions are not needed just to-day, they may be to-morrow, and somewhere they are needed to-day."[14]

Clara received this gold, Masonic pin from her father when she started her Civil War work.

During this time, Clara realized there were two necessities. First, there should be organization for the collection and distribution of items. Second, there was a need for advertising. Clara believed people would give, once they knew there was a need.

In February of 1862, Clara was called back to Oxford, Massachusetts, as her father was dying. Staying there for more than a month, she had many conversations with him about the problems of war. She mentioned the soldiers she had seen in Washington hospitals who needed supplies; but, her great concern was for those soldiers who suffered or lost their lives due to faulty transportation from the battlefield area to the hospitals in Washington. She felt that men needed more help on the battlefields. Her father was a very sympathetic listener, being a veteran of the Indian Wars himself. Clara asked her father if he thought she should go to the front. Later, she recalled his answer when she wrote, "As a patriot he bade me serve my country with all I had, even my life if need be; as the daughter of an accepted Mason he bade me seek and comfort the afflicted everywhere, and as a Christian he charged me to honor God and love mankind."[15] After their discussion, her father presented her with his gold, Masonic badge. Later she wrote, "My father gave it to me when I started for the front, and I have no doubt that it protected me on many an occasion."[16]

Prior to her father's death at age eighty-eight, Clara wrote the Governor of Massachusetts asking permission to go to Roanoke Island so she could be with General Burnside's men. She said in "his noble command are upwards of forty young men who in former days were my pupils."[17] The governor responded favorably to Clara's request but said he first needed to get a required recommendation from a Dr. Alfred Hitchcock. Unfortunately for Clara, Dr. Hitchcock did not believe that the battlefield was the place for women. He wrote, "I do not think at the present time Miss Barton had better undertake to go to Burnside's Division to act as a nurse."

In May, Clara returned to Washington and remained adamant in her desire to go to the front. Eventually, she obtained permission. How she obtained the many passes historians still do not know. The passes were quite unusual as most did not limit her to time or destination. For example on July 11, 1862, Surgeon-General of the United States, William A. Hammond, wrote, "Miss C.H. Barton has permission to go upon the sick transports in any direction – for the purpose of distributing comforts for the sick and wounded – and nursing them, always subject to the direction of the surgeon in charge." Another pass, written by

Quartermaster Col. D. H. Rucker, stated, ". . . that permission be given this lady and friend to pass to and from Acquia Creek on Government transports at all times when she may wish to visit the sick and hospitals, etc., with such stores as she may wish to take for the comfort of the sick and wounded."[18] Throughout the war, Clara managed to succeed in gaining access to the political and military authorities. This enabled her to move freely and get needed support and supplies.

After getting the passes, Clara did not rush to the front, but instead she returned to New England and visited New York, New Jersey, and Massachusetts requesting provisions. After returning to Washington, she went on her first expedition, Sunday, August 3, 1862. This time she took two assistants, Anna Carver and Cornelius Welles. Anna was from Philadelphia and a known "prominent war worker." Welles was a Baptist minister and a former missionary to South America. It was said he never minded taking orders from Clara and was eager to serve her "in any way."[19] During this journey, Clara and her crew would take supplies to Union forces in Stafford and those occupying Fredericksburg. Not wanting anything to happen to the provisions, Clara, who was now forty years old, hopped upon the wagon and sat beside the mule driver as the load was carted to the dock. A tugboat took her from Washington to Aquia Landing where she was greeted by a quartermaster. She stayed all night and at Monday's light she traveled on the Union railroad to Falmouth Station. From the station, Clara went to the elegant eighteenth century manor, the Lacy House which overlooked the colonial

The Lacy House, today known as Chatham, was used as a Union headquarters before and during the Battle of Fredericksburg. During and after the battle, it was also used as a hospital.

town of Fredericksburg. After breakfast she traveled across a suspension bridge which hung above the Rappahannock River and took supplies to the general hospital which was located in a woolen factory in Fredericksburg. It was here where she observed her first amputation.[20] The next day she found the 21st Massachusetts and distributed the rest of the supplies. Finding that more were needed, she returned to Washington Tuesday night. Later, Clara went straight to the Sanitary Commission and found a sympathetic ear. She was able to get supplies not only for the 21st Massachusetts but also for the 8th and 11th Connecticut Regiments.

A few days later, Clara went to Culpeper after the Battle of Cedar Mountain. Furnished with supplies from the Sanitary Commission, Clara, for "five days and nights with three hours' sleep," cared for 1,465 wounded. In her diary she stated that she cared for not only the injured Union but also Confederate troops.

At the end of that same month, after the Second Battle of Bull Run, Clara went by train to Manassas. She described the train as lacking many seats, platforms, or steps with just a side door and a window. She had to sit on boxes and barrels of "generous gifts" so she could look out the window. Once there, Clara was shocked to see that the ground was covered with hay and injured men were laying upon it for acres. More wounded kept pouring in. She wrote "…within fifteen minutes from the time of our arrival we were preparing food and dressing wounds."[21] A Pennsylvania surgeon, Dr. James Dunn, was there and was in dire need of bandages, salves, and dressing. He was so pleased when Clara provided him with needed supplies that he wrote his wife saying, "I thought that night if heaven ever sent out a homely angel, she must be one her assistance was so timely."[22]

Barely able to catch her breath, Clara heard about another Union loss at the Battle of Chantilly and departed immediately. She knelt down by one of the injured soldiers and he immediately buried his head in the folds of her dress. He asked if she knew him and said, "I am Charley Hamilton who used to carry your satchel home from school!" Clara recalled, "My faithful pupil, poor Charley. That mangled right arm would never carry a satchel again."[23] Clara wrote about many such heart-wrenching experiences she had encountered in just a few weeks' time. Clara endured rainy, dark, dreary, muddy nights and witnessed death, maiming, suffering, blood and tears. She became frustrated that she was not able to go to the battlefield before the action occurred. She always had to wait until the battle was over. If only she could be there immediately and help; perhaps more men would not be losing their lives. Staying in Washington frustrated her too, for she witnessed fevers, infections and gangrene in the hospitals. She thought; if only the men were treated earlier.

Hearing there was going to be a fight at Harper's Ferry, Clara loaded a wagon with supplies. With male helpers, she headed toward Maryland. Her wagon encountered a train of army wagons "at least ten miles in length." Many weary and sick men were falling by the side of the road. Clara immediately cut up bread and gave it to the "pale, haggard wrecks as they sat by the roadside."[24] Clara's advance information about Harper's Ferry came too late. The number of the wounded had not been that great and many of the wounded had already been taken to Frederick, Maryland. Leaving Harper's Ferry, she suddenly came upon the battlefield of South Mountain. She decided then and there her new motto would be "Follow the Cannon." She arrived at Antietam Creek prior to the battle and immediately went to work as soon as the first man was wounded. She did not leave the field until every soldier was cared for. At the end, Clara's supplies were exhausted, as was she. Fatigue, as well as a fever, set in. She returned to Washington the middle of September and stayed there several months gathering strength and supplies.

Later on in her life, Clara talked about the eight to ten men who were her drivers and helpers at Harper's Ferry, South Mountain and Antietam. They were not soldiers but were civilians employed by the government. At first, the men resented the fact they would be under the leadership of a woman. Later, the men realized that Clara was truly there to help the soldiers. Clara described the men. "Drovers, butchers, hucksters, mule-breakers, probably not one of them had ever passed an hour in what could be termed "ladies' society," in his life . . . They were brave and skillful, understood their business to perfection, but had no art." There was mutual admiration. Clara recalled, "These men remained with me six months through frost and snow and march and camp and battle; and nursed the sick, dressed the wounded, soothed the dying, and buried the dead; and if possible grew kinder and gentler every day."[25]

CLARA BARTON
From portrait taken in Civil War and authorized by her as the one she wished to be remembered by

This image of Clara was created from a portrait taken during the Civil War. She authorized it as the "one she wanted to be remembered by."

The first part of December in 1862, Clara packed up supplies and returned to Stafford via steamer from D.C. Upon arriving at Aquia Landing, she was pleasantly surprised to find out that her old friend from the 21st Massachusetts, Major Hall, was quartermaster. The boat was unloaded and she spent the evening reminiscing with the major. The next day, Clara traveled via railroad to Falmouth Station. She was shocked to see the transformation of Stafford County that had taken place since her visit in August. Now trees were cut down for the over 135,000 Union soldiers to create their shelters, build their corduroy roads, cook their food, and keep warm. She saw tent villages that were constructed on the barren land along the railroad trail.

General Sturgis, originally of the 21st Massachusetts, had his ambulance waiting for Clara at the station. The 21st Massachusetts truly loved Clara. In their regimental history it was written of Clara:

> Our true friend, Miss Clara Barton, however, a 21st woman to the backbone, was now permanently associated with the regiment, and, with two four-mule covered wagons, which by her untiring efforts she kept well supplied with delicacies in the way of food and articles of clothing, was a ministering angel to our sick. General Sturgis kindly ordered a detail from the regiment of drivers and assistants about her wagons. And this true, noble woman, never sparing herself or failing in her devotion to our suffering men, always maintained her womanly dignity, and won the lasting respect and love of our officers and men.[26]

Clara left Falmouth Station and traveled to Sturgis' headquarters at the farmhouse of James M.S. Threshley. (It was located near present-day Grafton Village.) There Clara had supper and a "splendid serenade." She later wrote, "I don't know how we could have had a warmer 'welcome home,' as the officers termed it."[27] That night, Clara and a Miss G. shared a room in the farm house. (Historians have yet to identify Miss G.) Clara wrote that, despite snow being on the ground, she wished for a tent, floor, and stove so she could stay by her wagons rather than stay in "a rebel house."[28]

The next morning Clara traveled for a second time to the "stately mansion," the Lacy House. This time she was shocked to see that, by the Rappahannock, a "little canvas city grew up in a night upon its banks."[29] She also observed over 150 pieces of artillery which were lined up on Stafford Heights and pointed toward Fredericksburg.[30] Some historians believe Clara was probably at the Lacy House during the day and stayed at the Threshley farm at night. She witnessed troops who waited impatiently for Burnside to give them orders. Burnside, on the other hand, was waiting for pontoon trains (wagons with teams, boats, and wooden planks) to arrive from Maryland and D.C. so he could construct floating bridges for his men to traverse the Rappahannock into Fredericksburg.

Finally, the bridges arrived. On Thursday, December 11th, Clara stood on the upper, or "second portico" of the Lacy House and watched as the engineers from the 7th Michigan tried to construct a pontoon bridge directly below the Lacy House. She said a, "few boats were fastened and the men marched quickly on with timbers and planks." Then, "a rain of musket balls has swept their ranks and the brave fellows lie level with the bridge or float down the stream."[31] "Then rolled the thunder and the fire. For two long hours the shot and shell hurled through the roofs" of Fredericksburg. Despite the Union cannon firing, men "fell like grass before the scythe." Then the Federal troops realized that there were rebel sharpshooters located in the cellars of town. Burnside yelled to the men to, "Man the boats." Paddling in the awkward vessels across the Rappahannock, the Union soldiers got out of the boats and attacked the sharpshooters so the bridges could be completed.[32]

Clara witnessed the Union forces struggling to build the pontoon bridge directly below the Lacy House.

At two o'clock the next morning Clara wrote this letter to her cousin, Elvira Stone, of the impending fighting:

Dec 12th 1862 - 2 oclock AM

Dear Cousin Vira:

Five minutes' time with you, and God only knows what that five minutes might be worth to the – may be – doomed thousands sleeping around me. It is the night before a "battle." The enemy, Fredericksburg, and its mighty entrenchments lie before us – the river between. At to-morrow's dawn our troops will essay to cross and the guns of the enemy will sweep their frail bridges at every breath. The moon is shining through the soft haze with a brightness almost prophetic; for the last half-hour I have stood alone in the awful stillness of its glimmering light gazing upon the strange, sad scene around me striving to say, "Thy will, O God, be done." The camp-fires blaze with unwonted brightness, the sentry's tread is still but quick, the scores of little shelter tents are dark and still as death; no wonder, for, as I gazed sorrowfully upon them, I thought I could almost hear the slow flap of the grim messenger's wings as one by one he sought and selected his victims for the morning's sacrifice. Sleep, weary ones, sleep and rest for to-morrow's toil! Oh, sleep and visit in dreams once more the loved ones nestling at home! They may yet live to dream of you, cold, lifeless, and bloody; but this dream, soldier, is thy last; paint it brightly, dream it well. Oh Northern mothers, wives, and sisters, all unconscious of the peril of the hour, would to Heaven that I could bear for you the concentrated woe which is so soon to follow; would that Christ would teach my soul a prayer that would plead to the Father for grace sufficient for you all! God pity and strengthen you every one. Mine are not the only waking hours; the light yet burns brightly in our kind-hearted General's tent, where he pens what may be a last farewell to his wife and children, and thinks sadly of his fated men. Already the roll of the moving artillery is sounding in my ears. The battle draws near and I must catch one hour's sleep for to-day's labor. Good-night, and heaven grant you strength for your more peaceful and terrible, but not less weary, days than mine.[33]

Yours in love
Clara

The letter to her cousin sheds light on Clara's deep feelings and shows her compassion. Some of Clara's letters, however, help paint a picture of the war. For example, the following letter, written several months after the Battle of Fredericksburg, describes what it was like at the Lacy House shortly after the river assault and crossing. Clara wrote this thank you letter to the mother of a little girl who sent a box of fruit for the troops.

I opened your boxes during the early part of the bombardment of Fredericksburg and finding little Mary's gift I took it with me to the Lacy House the following day. The sadly wounded of the brave Michigan 7th were lying there with those who had fallen on the bridge, and in the bloody streets of Fredericksburg and while the house was reeling and tottering to its foundation, with the terrible recoil of our own guns, the enemies solid shot and bursting shell were plowing the ground all around us killing wounded men at the door. I opened little Mary's bag of delicious fruit and cut the apples in quarters and divided them among the poor suffering men lying upon the floors already slippery with blood. The one orange I gave to a man shot in the neck who could not drink, only hold liquids in his mouth, and was dying of thirst [sic] if ever a *little girl's* labors were hallowed by prayers and blessings surely your little daughters were, for all receive them as the gift of a child, and strong men *became children* at the thought [sic] many a man's thoughts turned to his own little daughter in the peaceful northern home he was destined neve[r] to see. Please give my thanks and love to little Mary and tell her that I expect to see her if I live to come to Bordentown.[34]

The next day, December 13th, the Union troops moved through town only to be shot down by the Confederates on Marye's Heights. While Burnside was delayed by the late arrival of the pontoon boats, General Robert E. Lee had taken advantage of the situation by establishing impenetrable defenses on the heights beyond the city. He had his corps commanders, James Longstreet and "Stonewall" Jackson, move into position with 78,000 troops. They waited on the heights overlooking Fredericksburg and defended at the Sunken Road's stone wall. Firing down on the advancing Union soldiers, the Confederates caused many casualties and took many lives. That morning at 10 o'clock, Clara received a crumpled, bloody slip of paper, from a courier. It was "a request from the lion-hearted old surgeon on the opposite shore, establishing his hospitals in the very jaws of death." The note said, "Come to me. Your place is here." The men who worked with Clara eight weeks before, decided to accompany her across the Rappahannock as did her assistant, Cornelius Wells. She wrote, ". . . in twenty minutes we were rocking across the swaying bridge, the water hissing with shot on either side."[35]

Clara found a devastated Fredericksburg.

When Clara got to the other side of the river, an officer assisted her over debris at the end of the bridge. She said that, "while our hands were raised in the act of stepping down, a piece of an exploding shell hissed through between us, just below our arms, carrying away a portion of both the skirts of his coat and my dress, rolling along the ground a few rods from us like a harmless pebble into the water."[36] Clara made it to a hospital in a church to assist the surgeon, only to find that in less than a half-hour the kind officer who helped her at the bridge, was brought in dead.

On Saturday, Clara traveled from hospital to hospital -- meaning that she traveled from house to house or house to church, as most structures in town, including the city hall and factories, were being used as hospitals. On one of her mad dashes through town she was stopped by Union Provost-Marshal-General Marsena Patrick while he was patrolling the streets on horseback. Not recognizing Clara and thinking she was a resident of Fredericksburg, he bent down from his saddle and said, "You are alone and in great danger, Madam. Do you not want protection?" Thanking him she said that she believed she was one of the best protected women in the United States. Soldiers nearby set up a cheer and responded by saying, "That's so! That's so!" Soldiers, also in the street, joined the chorus. Clara wrote, "The gallant old General, taking in the situation, bowed low in his bared head, saying, as he galloped away, 'I believe you are right, Madam.'"[37]

On Sunday afternoon, while still in Fredericksburg, an officer "came hurriedly" to ask Clara to go to a church to take care of a man who was covered in dry blood. The officer was afraid of suffocation. Seizing a "basin of water and a sponge" Clara knelt by the dying man to clean and comfort him. Later she wrote of the experience. "After some hours' labor, I began to recognize features. They seemed familiar. With what impatience I wrought. Finally my hand wiped away the last obstruction. An eye opened, and there to my gaze was the sexton of my old home church!"[38]

Historians believe that Clara discovered her hometown church sexton in the Fredericksburg Baptist Church.

Clara went into several Fredericksburg churches and buildings, like the City Hall, to tend the wounded. There is an historical marker outside The Presbyterian Church citing her achievements.

In Fredericksburg, Clara not only tended to men's wounds, but also helped supply their nourishment. She and Cornelius Wells, established a soup kitchen. The kitchen prepared soup for hundreds for many days.[39]

Returning to the Lacy House, Clara said twelve hundred wounded men crowded into the mansion with just twelve rooms. However, official reports say there were just under 300.[40] Later Clara wrote, "I cannot tell you the numbers but some hundreds of the worst wounded men I have ever seen, lying on little hay on floors or in tents . . . "[41] Regardless of the exact number, men covered every square foot of the house including stair landings. Some were even placed on cupboard shelves. A man considered himself fortunate if his head were lying underneath a table, for he knew he would not be stepped on.[42] Outside, Clara noticed fifty wounded men were lying on the snowy ground and on the porticos of the house. They were going to freeze if something could not be done before they were brought into the house for surgery. Immediately, Clara ordered a chimney of an abandoned outbuilding torn down. Then she had the bricks heated by a fire. Wrapping the freezing men in Union wool blankets, Clara's helpers place the hot bricks beside the wounded throughout the night.[43]

In the crowded house, Clara noticed a young boy from the 7th Michigan who was propped up in the corner of a room. Being shot through the lungs, he was unable to lie down and had difficulty breathing and swallowing. Clara asked his name and address, as she did most of the injured men. With much trouble, he said his last name was Faulkner and he was from Ohio. Just at that time another boy came in with a similar injury. Thinking that Faulkner was not breathing anymore, she said once he was removed, the other patient could take his place in the corner. When men attempted to move him, he astonished everyone when he opened his eyes and said he did not want to budge from that place. Amazingly he stayed in the corner for two weeks. Clara said Faulkner was "a mere bundle of skin and bones . . . he was wrapped in a blanket and taken away in an ambulance to Washington, with a bottle of milk punch in his blouse, the only nourishment he could take."[44] (Milk punch was usually a mixture of condensed milk, water, and whiskey or rum.)

Just as Clara had done for Faulkner, she tried to keep records of the men at the Lacy House, even if it was just scribbling notes on her pocket diary. She attempted to record rank, name, and address for the living. For those who had died at the manor, she took notes denoting the manner and time of death and attempted to obtain their units and disposition of remains. Rebel troops at the Lacy House were also recorded. For example, she listed a Confederate prisoner as: "Capt. Thomas Wm. Thurman Co. D 13 Miss. Decatur Miss, leg amputated. Parents in Georgia. 23 yers.old."[45] Clara's detailed notes would prove to be a very helpful tool for family and friends in both the North and South.

As Welles and Clara had done in Fredericksburg, they established a soup kitchen at the Lacy House. Clara found many other tasks to do at the house. She would care for post-surgery patients by placing pillows under amputated body parts, giving the Surgeon General's liquor when patients needed relief from pain, cradling men in her arms, and even singing to them, if necessary. For example, a Lt. Edgar M. Newcomb of Massachusetts was lying on a sofa hemorrhaging from his wounds. His brother, Charlie, and Clara knelt by his side and quoted scripture and sang comforting hymns. The dying lieutenant believed Clara to be his mother and she "kindly favored the illusion." After many hours he died. Later Clara wrote, "When I rose from the side of the couch, I wrung the blood from the bottom of my clothing, before I could step, for the weight about my feet."[46]

One of the soldiers on the grounds of the Lacy House fell when he received a fragment from an exploding shell that lodged in his ankle. Unfortunately, it hit an artery, so blood spurted everywhere. Dragged into the mansion by fellow soldiers, Clara immediately tied a handkerchief around his leg to stop the flow of blood. The grateful man was so appreciative of Clara's speedy efforts that, whenever he saw her around the house, he would say, "You saved my life."[47]

By this time, Clara and Miss G., were not the only women assisting at the Lacy House. Others, too, had come to help, but Clara still retained the distinction of being the only female volunteer nurse and relief worker in Fredericksburg during the height of the battle.[48]

The Falmouth Station was located appropriately where the Fraternal Order of Eagles Lodge on Cool Springs Road is today.

On December 16th, wounded men were being evacuated from hospitals and from around the Falmouth Railroad Station. Clara tried to prepare her patients for the ambulance ride from the Lacy House to the railroad station. She would mix "hot toddies" for them and promise to visit them in Washington. The journey aboard the train to Aquia Landing was a very treacherous one, for the injured men often had to ride on open platform cars and endure freezing weather. The bumpy journey could even open some wounds. Once they arrived at Aquia Landing they received good care, as the Sanitary Commission gave them hot food, canned milk, blankets, shirts, and woolen clothing. From there they would be placed on steamers and taken to hospitals to Washington

Clara's forty-first birthday, Christmas Day, was spent at the Lacy House while still moving men on stretchers and in ambulances to Falmouth station. She accompanied Sergeant Thomas Plunkett, one of "her boys" from the 21st Massachusetts, to the Falmouth Station. Plunkett was a brave soldier who kept holding the colors of the 21st even though a shell shattered both his arms during the battle.[49] After all the wounded had been evacuated, Clara and her assistants took down their tents and packed up for their journey D.C. By this time all Clara's supplies had been consumed. She secured a pass from General Sturgis and returned home via steamer from Aquia Landing.

On the last day of the year, Clara's boat docked at Washington's Sixth Street Wharf. She then had to trudge through "ankle-deep" mud in order to catch a streetcar home. Walking up the long stairway to her room, she sat down on a box that was sitting in the center and looked at herself – "shoeless, gloveless, ragged, and blood-stained, a new sense of desolation and pity and sympathy and weariness, all blended, swept over me with irresistible force, and, perfectly overpowered."[50] Etched on her brain were the scenes of Fredericksburg and the Lacy House, "never to be erased." She could still see the fires of Fredericksburg and hear the cannons thundering in her ear and the groans of the wounded and dying. She wept. Later she noticed the strange box on which she sat. Opening it rapidly, she found a letter underneath paper wrappings that said, "From friends in Oxford and Worcester." Then she lifted out, "one after another, hoods, shoes, boots, gloves, skirts, handkerchiefs, collars, linen" and a beautiful dress. She wept again, this time for a different reason. She realized while she was toiling away down south, her friends up north were working to create lovely clothes for her. When writing a thank you note for the gifts she scribed, "Again, I re-dedicated myself to my little work of humanity, pledging before God all that I have, all that I am, all that I can, and all that I hope to be, to the cause of *Justice* and *Mercy* and *Patriotism*, my *Country*, and my *God*."[51]

By the middle of January, Colonel Rucker of the Quartermaster's Department informed Clara that the Army of the Potomac was going to move out again and that there may be another battle. General Burnside was not content to admit defeat and planned to have his army move west on Warrenton Road and then south along Bank's Ford Peninsula to attack Lee's left flank. (Today, that means they would travel along U.S. Highway 17 and turn left by Celebrate Virginia's Cannon Ridge Golf Course and cross over the Rappahannock River.) Rucker requested that Clara return to Stafford if she was able. He provided her with flour, bread, two new tents, and a new stove.[52] She looked over the supplies and found that medical supplies were in short supply. Not having enough money to buy supplies of her own, she went to an old friend, Massachusetts Senator Henry Wilson. As a matter of fact, Wilson had visited her when she was at the Lacy House the month before. She requested he supply her with "medical stores."[53] This was contrary to Clara's former operations, for this was the first time she asked the War Department for goods instead of just relying on women's aid societies.

On January 18th, Clara and her assistant, Cornelius Welles, returned to Stafford. Two days later, the Army of Potomac streamed out of Falmouth following Burnside's orders to attack Lee. Unfortunately, for the Union troops, it started to rain with a freezing downpour. The rain lasted several days creating deep mud. Wagons, cannons, ambulances, pontoon boats, horses, mules, and troops got stuck in the quagmire. Burnside aborted his plan and had the troops return to their old camps, many of which had previously been destroyed following his own orders. Dejected, the men trudged back. After the failed "Mud March," Clara and Wells had decided to return to Washington on the 23rd. Back at home, she worked on answering the myriad of letters that had collected when she was in Stafford during December and part of January.

Clara was in Stafford during Burnside's disastrous Mud March.

A few months later, Clara received a message from Lincoln Hospital that the men of Ward 17 wanted to see her. Upon entering the ward she was shocked to see seventy men salute her, as best as they could while attempting to stand. Later, she wrote about the thrilling confrontation:

> Every man had left his blood in Fredericksburg – every one was from the Lacy house. My hand had dressed every wound – many of them in the first terrible moments of agony. I had prepared their food in the snow and winds of December and fed them like children. How dear they had grown to me in their sufferings, and the three great cheers that greeted my entrance into that hospital ward were dearer than the applause. I would not exchange their memory for the wildest hurrahs that ever greeted the ear of conqueror or king.[54]

A young man walked up to her. She said she recognized his face, but couldn't recall him until he said, "I am Riley Faulkner, of the 7th Michigan. I didn't die, and the milk punch lasted all the way to Washington!"[55]

The spring of 1863 found Clara thinking about traveling to Charleston, South Carolina. She felt "her Army of the Potomac" was now reasonably well cared for and that there was probably a greater need for her in the South based on rumors she had heard in Washington, D.C. There was also a personal reason, as she wished to establish communication with her brother, Stephen, who was in North Carolina. Confirmation of Clara making the correct decision came when she heard her other brother, David, would be stationed near Charleston.

Since Clara's service was unsolicited and voluntary, she needed to get permission to travel to South Carolina with supplies. As her cousin, William Barton, later wrote, "She was not an army nurse, and had no intention of becoming one. The system of army nurses was under the direct supervision of Dorothea Dix."[56] Dorothea Dix was twenty-nine years older than Clara and had established a system of nurses for hospitals. Clara held Miss Dix in the highest regard and never, at any time, wished to interfere with her system. However, Clara felt her place was on the battlefield and, whenever necessary, she would be there to help surgeons.

On April 7th, 1863, Clara arrived at Hilton Head, South Carolina. She heard, upon disembarking, that the battle, that supposedly was to take place in Charleston, had been postponed. Therefore, Clara distributed her perishable supplies. She discovered most of the wounded and ill were already in hospitals and were being taken care of by the Sanitary Commission. Clara's reputation had preceded her to South Carolina. She received visits from local hospital nurses, flowers from different officers, and numerous band serenades. Officers at headquarters even invited her to go horseback riding with them. After procuring a riding skirt, she joined them practically every morning. Not wishing to waste her time waiting for battle, she taught some young black boys to read and, whenever possible, comforted homesick soldiers. She also tried to nurse soldiers who were dying of malaria. Clara, however, was getting antsy after nine months in the South. She wanted to play a more active role, so she returned to Washington in January of 1864.

The first four months of the year found Clara attempting to sock-pile supplies and hoping to go wherever needed. Early in May, she heard about the fighting at The Wilderness and Spotsylvania Court House, where wounded troops were streaming into Fredericksburg. Unfortunately, there were 7,000-8,000 wounded men and only about 30-40 surgeons to take care of them. On May 11th she started her returned to Stafford for a fourth time. Carrying only coffee and two kettles, she boarded the steamer *Wenonah* in the afternoon at the Seventh Street Wharf along with other volunteers. She planned to assess the situation once there and then return for the needed supplies.

Instead of stopping at Aquia Landing, the *Wenonah* went around Marlborough Point and on to Belle Plain on Potomac Creek. Clara's usual routine of disembarking at Aquia Landing and moving by rail to Falmouth was not possible due to the previous destruction of the rail line. Clara arrived the afternoon of the 12th at Belle Plain. She witnessed a bustling harbor full of all sorts of transport, supply, and troop ships. Since Belle Plain was much shallower than Aquia Landing, supplies and troops had to be loaded and unloaded by barges from anchored vessels. There was only one narrow wharf at the Stafford site. (Another wharf existed, also named Belle Plain, in adjacent King George County.) The scene was hectic and at times chaotic: wounded men were awaiting placement on ships to take them to hospitals in Washington; supplies were waiting to be unloaded and loaded onto wagons; and passengers were waiting to arrive and depart.

Clara encountered mud and chaos at Belle Plain.

It was pouring down rain, so Clara and the rest of the passengers remained on board the *Wenonah*. The next morning Clara departed the steamer and walked off the wharf. There she observed, what she called, the "peculiar geographic location" of Belle Plain. She found a "narrow ridge" on the left bank and Potomac Creek on the right bank. "On the left, the hills towered up almost to a mountain height." She saw that there was just a very narrow road leading out to Fredericksburg, "leaving a level space or basin of an area of a fourth of a mile, directly in front of the landing." This crowded area revealed a shocking sight. Red mud and the wounded were everywhere. Wagons were "sunk to the hub in mud, and stalled where they could not get out, while men groaned and died and maggots crawled in their wounds."[57]

Meanwhile in Fredericksburg, thousands of wounded from the Wilderness battle were still streaming into town. Once seen by surgeons, they were "taken away in army wagons across ten miles of alternate hills, and hollows, stumps, roots, and mud!" to Belle Plain.[58]

Clara stepped onto a ridge at Belle Plain and observed:

> Standing in this plain of mortar-mud were at least two hundred six-mule army wagons, crowded full of wounded men waiting to be taken upon the boats for Washington. They had driven from Fredericksburg that morning. Each driver had gotten his wagon as far as he could for those in front of and about him had stopped.[59]

Clara also noticed the Christian Commission had erected several tents on the ridge and were probably contemplating what to do, as it was still raining. A clergyman from the commission approached Clara, and they talked about what they could do to help the wounded. Based on her experience, Clara realized the troops were very hungry and must be fed, but the man said that he had "a great deal of clothing and reading matter, but no food in any quantity, excepting crackers." Clara informed him she had coffee, so between the two of them they could give hot coffee and crackers.[60] The clergyman was doubtful this could be accomplished, but Clara showed him where they could start a fire with brush. Then the gentleman said, "Our crackers are in barrels, and we have neither basket nor box. How can we carry them?" Ingeniously, Clara created aprons using table-cloths which "fastened all four of the corners to the waist, and pinned the sides, thus leaving one hand for kettle of coffee and one free, to administer it." Once ready to deliver food, the minister asked, "How are we to get to them?" She immediately started walking in the mud and "with a backward glance . . . saw the good man tighten his grasp upon his apron and take his first step into military life."[61]

After delivering crackers and coffee, Clara traveled the ten miles into Fredericks-burg and was further shocked to witness even greater horrors. She heard a Union captain, who was staying in a lovely mansion in town, say the refined people in Fredericksburg should not be compelled to open their homes to "these dirty, lousy, common soldiers . . ."[62] Therefore, men were crowded in the streets. Clara's own words depict the horrible conditions she encountered:

> . . . I saw, crowded into one old sunken hotel, lying helpless upon its bare, wet, bloody floors, five hundred fainting men hold up their cold, bloodless, dingy hands, as I passed, and beg me in Heaven's name for a cracker to keep them from starving (and I had none); or to give them a cup that they might have something to drink water from, if they could get it (and I had no cup and could get none); till I saw two hundred six-mule army wagons in a line, ranged down the street to headquarters, and reaching so far out on the Wilderness road that I never found the end of it; every wagon crowded with wounded men, stopped, standing in the rain and mud, wrenched back and forth by the restless, hungry animals all night from four o'clock in the afternoon till eight next morning and how much longer I know not. The dark spot in the mud under many a wagon, told only too plainly where some poor fellow's life had dripped out in those dreadful hours.[63]

Realizing something must be done immediately, Clara rushed back to Belle Plain on a light army wagon, through mud and mire, and got on a steam tug returning to Washington at dusk. She contacted her friend, Senator Henry Wilson. He met Clara at eight that evening and was appalled to hear what was going on. Wilson, a member of the powerful committee on the conduct of the war, wielded signifi-cant power to jostle the Army bureaucracy. Two hours later found the senator at the War Department saying, "One of two things will have to be done – either you will send some one tonight with the power to investigate and correct the abuses of our wounded men at Fredericksburg, or the Senate will send some one tomorrow."[64] Investigators were in town the next morning by ten, to Clara's great delight. "At noon the wounded men were fed from the food of the city and the houses were opened to the '*dirty, lousy* soldiers' of the Union Army."[65]

About a week later, on May 21st, Clara returned by steamer to Stafford bringing with her "carloads of supplies." Aboard the steamer, she met a Mrs. Myers whose husband, a captain in the Fifth Army Corps, was in a Fredericksburg hospital recovering from a shot through the lungs. Clara discovered that Mrs. Myers was from Massachusetts and did what she could to befriend her. Reaching Belle Plain about one o'clock, she had a squad of men unload her stores. By three, she and Mrs. Myers "got off in a spring wagon piled almost to the top with boxes." Every time the wagon reached a hill, the ladies had to disembark so the horses could make it up the inclines. It was dark by the time they reached Fredericksburg. The first people they found were members of the Christian Commission. One went with Mrs. Myers to help find her husband. A Captain Jones procured supper for

Clara and arranged for her to "sleep with a secesh family" whose husband was in the "rebel army." Clara went upstairs and wrote that "a little Negro working came to my room and insisted upon taking off my boots and rubbing my feet which she did most perfectly." The next morning Clara arose and paid the owner of the house fifty cents for her lodging and gave the little girl fifteen cents for rubbing her feet. Clara had her supplies unloaded and went around town. She found Mrs. Myers in a private home by the Baptist Church, which was being used as a hospital. Unfortunately, she discovered that the captain was "sinking fast." In the house's parlor, she was pleased to find her cousin, Ned Barton. In another hospital, Clara found another cousin, George Barton. Evacuations for the walking wounded were taking place in town. Those most seriously wounded remained. From a letter, written by a nurse, we know that Clara tended to these soldiers wearing a blue dress and a white apron. She encouraged those lying there by singing *Rally Round the Flag Boys*.[66] Later that evening she fixed dinner for a Dr. Lamb. While washing the dishes she heard from afar the train whistle from Falmouth railroad station. She realized Aquia Landing had been repaired, and trains were again running. Before going to bed that evening, Clara wrote that hearing the train whistle "sent a thrill of joy through us all. No more carting wounded men to Belle Plain."[67] No more being stuck in red mud and "no more jolting in army wagons!"[68]

This picture of Clara, during the Civil War, was taken by Matthew Brady.

The May trip was Clara's last trip to the Stafford-Fredericksburg area. In June she was appointed Superintendent of the Department of Nurses for the Army of the James. During this time she assumed other duties. Her cousin William wrote, "She was a head-nurse, in charge of the hospitals of an entire army corps. Not only so, but she was on occasion chief cook and purveyor of pie and gingerbread, and picked codfish and New England boiled dinners so like what the soldiers loved…"[69] Later he wrote that Clara "… did not long continue in hospital service after the immediate need was passed. With the firing of the last gun she returned to Washington. One chapter in her career was closed. Another and important work was about to open…"[70]

While back in Washington, Clara received countless letters from families inquiring if she knew the whereabouts of their relatives. Clara discovered that out of the 315,555 graves of the Union soldiers, only 172,400 were identified. Additionally, there were "43,973 recorded deaths over and above the number of graves."[71] In March of 1865, Clara brought these facts to President Lincoln's attention and asked if an agency could be established for finding missing soldiers. Immediately, the president gave Clara permission to establish just such an agency. However, it took the War Department two months to set up headquarters in Annapolis. All she was given was a tent with furniture, stationery, clerks, and a fund for postage. She later moved her office to an apartment in Washington. After concerned citizens heard about the new agency, Clara received around one hundred inquiries a day. She worked tirelessly for four years and at the end believed that she had given information to over 22,000 families.

(In 1997, a three-story building at 437 7th NW Street in Washington, D.C., just eleven blocks from the White House, was scheduled to be demolished. In the attic, a tin sign with gold letters and a black background was found. It read: *Missing Soldiers Office, 3rd Story, Room 9, Miss Clara Barton*. Besides the sign, there were 20 boxes of books, letters, and men's clothing, dating from the 1860s. It is believed that Clara conducted her business in the apartment, and probably lived, immediately below the attic. Needless to say, the building was not destroyed. The third floor was preserved and the first two floors were renovated. With the help of the General Service Administration and The National Park Service, the apartment is now a museum open for visitors.)

While working with the agency, Clara heard about a young discharged prisoner, Dorence Atwater of Connecticut. While at Andersonville he took detailed records of prisoners and their deaths. His lists accounted for thirteen thousand Union soldiers in the year of 1865 alone. Being very interested, Clara asked Secretary of War Stanton if she and Dorence Atwater could go to Andersonville with helpers. There they would try to enclose the cemetery with a fence and mark each grave with a headboard. Together they made the area into a national cemetery and Clara had the honor of raising the United States flag commemorating the soldiers' sacrifices.

Clara was forty-five years old when she completed her Civil War crusade to account for the missing and dead. The next forty-five years of her life were filled with trips around the nation and around the world extending her relief efforts and telling her story in order to raise additional funds.

Starting in 1866, Clara gave nation-wide lectures about her Civil War experiences. She chose Dorence Atwater to be her assistant. Clara was able to command $75-$100 per lecture. Sometimes she was given extra money for travel. Some of the money she gave to various charities, but she was able to keep much for herself. These funds became a basis for her later work. She lectured for over two years giving approximately 200 presentations. While giving a talk in Maine she lost her voice, attributing it to fatigue. Hoping to regain her health, she left for Europe in September of 1869. While there, she learned of the International Convention of Geneva – the Red Cross. In 1870, she volunteered to serve the International Red Cross during the Franco-Prussian War.

1871 found Clara in Paris and Lyon, France doing relief work. Two years later, in poor health, she returned to the United States. She became very frustrated that no one could diagnose her illness. Today authorities believe she probably was suffering from exhaustion and a bleeding ulcer.[72] In 1876, she moved to a sanitarium in Dansville, New York, where she was placed on a healthy diet and

Taken in 1878, this photo shows Clara wearing a Red Cross pin she received for her service with the German Red Cross during the Franco-Prussian War.

obtained needed rest. In 1877, based on her favorable evaluation of the Red Cross in the Franco-Prussian War, Clara started lobbying for an American branch of the Red Cross. Thanks to her tireless lobbying, her efforts were finally successful. Four years later, in 1881, the American Association of the Red Cross was formed and Clara was elected President. The first contributions of this new association were giving supplies to the victims of Michigan forest fires.

In March of 1882, President Chester A. Arthur signed the Treaty of Geneva, making the United States a member of the International Red Cross. In the spring of that year, through part of 1883, Clara directed Red Cross relief work during the Mississippi River flooding.

Never sitting still, Clara briefly served as superintendent of the Woman's Reformatory Prison at Sherborn, Massachusetts. During her time there, her Red Cross work suffered, as she could only work on it during the mornings. Therefore, she remained in that position for only eight months.

In February of 1884, Clara led in relief work during the Ohio River floods. In August of that year she served as the first female United States ambassador attending the International Conference of the Red Cross in Geneva, Switzerland.

For the next three years, from 1885-1888, Clara directed relief efforts in Texas during times of drought; in Illinois after a tornado; and in Florida after a yellow fever epidemic.

Some of her work was international, as in 1892, she provided famine relief for Russia. In 1893, she assisted victims in the South Carolina Sea Islands after a horrific hurricane and tidal wave. 1896 found Clara in Armenia helping the sick and starving. The next year, in 1897, Clara made the warehouse, which was constructed six years before in Glen Echo, Maryland, her home and headquarters. She didn't stay there long, for in 1898, Clara was in Cuba assisting the wounded during the Spanish-American War. She stayed there until 1900. While there she met Theodore Roosevelt. Later that year, Clara returned to the states and directed relief work in Texas after a hurricane.

In 1902, Clara headed to St. Petersburg, Russia where she led the delegation from the United States to the International Conference of the Red Cross. It was during this visit that Clara went to Germany and visited Agnes Salm-Salm. Two years later, at the age of eighty-two, Clara resigned as president of the American National Red Cross and retired to her home in Glen Echo.

Clara resigned as president of the American Red Cross at the age of eighty-two.

Clara passed away on April 12, 1912, at her home. She was buried in the family cemetery plot in North Oxford, Massachusetts. Her cousin, Rev. William Barton, gave the eulogy at her service. Later, he summed up her influence in the world when he wrote:

> She knew personally every president from Lincoln to Roosevelt, and was acquainted with nearly every man of prominence in our national life. When she went abroad, her associates were people of high rank and wide influence in their respective countries. No American woman received more honor while she lived, either at home or abroad, and how worthily she bore these honors those know best who knew her best.[73]

Walt Whitman

The Good Gray Poet.

When the Civil War began, Walt Whitman was already well known in America as the author of the controversial book of poetry, *Leaves of Grass*. He was in his forties and did not enlist, but his younger brother, George Washington Whitman, did. Daily, Walt read the *New York Tribune* to discover what was happening to the Union forces. On Tuesday, December 16, 1862, his eyes glanced at an article which listed those who were wounded in the Battle of Fredericksburg. Under the 51st New York Volunteer Infantry was a "First Lieutenant G.W. Whitmore, Company D." Despite the misspelling Walt knew that this was his brother. He wanted to travel to Virginia immediately and see the extent of George's wounds, as he loved him so much.

Walter Whitman, Jr. was born in a small rural village of West Hills in Long Island, New York, on May 31, 1819. His father, a farmer, and mother, a housewife, had nine children in all. However, one son died in infancy. Walt, named after his father, had two other brothers with patriotic names like George. One was Andrew Jackson Whitman, and the other was Thomas Jefferson Whitman.

Walt was very close to his mother,
Louisa Van Velsor Whitman.

Walt was named after his father,
Walter Whitman, Sr.

When Walt was four years old the family moved to Brooklyn, as his father decided to switch careers and be a carpenter. He had hoped to construct small frame houses in the area. Walt said his father would say, "Oh! What a comfort it is to lie down on your own floor, a floor laid with your own hands, in a house which represents your own handiwork - cellar and walls and roof!"[1] Unfortunately, his father's business did not prosper and records show that in the ten years the family lived in Brooklyn, they moved at least seven times. Sometimes Walt would say of his childhood, "The time of my boyhood was a very restless and unhappy one. I did not know what to do."[2] At other times he recalled fond memories.

Probably due to his family's financial situation, Walt left school at the age of eleven to work as an office boy for two lawyers. His life opened up when one gave him a library card. Walt said that was, "the signal event of my life up to that time." Walt devoured books and was especially impressed by Cooper's novels and the *Arabian Nights*.

A year later, Walt became a printer's apprentice for the editor of the weekly *Long Island Patriot*. He learned how to typeset articles and, within a year's time, was writing and setting his own articles. At age thirteen, Walt's family moved back to Long Island, but he stayed on in Brooklyn as a compositor for the weekly newspaper the *Long-Island Star*. He remained there for three years and obtained firsthand experience in the expanding printing industry. He learned publication distribution knowledge and developed a substantial work-ethic. He read articles as they came in and was exposed to a wide variety of subjects and authors. He familiarized himself with such issues as temperance, tariffs, slavery, and antislavery.

Later, Walt spent one year as a compositor in the city of Manhattan. The great fire of August 12, 1835, which swept through the commercial district, had Whitman joining the safe refuge of his family. Returning to West Hills, Long Island, he discovered his father had sold the old Whitman home and one hundred acres. His family was now living in Norwich, so Walt took a job teaching school. Later, the family moved to West Babylon where his father took up farming again. Walt joined the family there. He took another teaching position to help with family finances. Whitman would remember fondly his time at Babylon which was near wetlands and water: "The shores of this bay, winter and summer, and my doings there in early life, are woven all through L[eaves] of G[rass]."[3] Eventually, Whitman moved around Long Island accepting various teaching jobs, but he returned frequently to Babylon using it as his home base.

When eighteen, Walt left his family and took teaching positions on Long Island at Long Swamp and later Smithtown. While in Smithtown he became active in a debating society. It was there, however, he decided to leave the teaching profession, travel to Huntington, and found his own weekly newspaper, the *Long-Islander*. His eight year-old brother, George, assisted him for a while. Walt's biographer, David Reynolds, wrote, "Whitman was publisher, editor, compositor, pressman, and distributor all at once."[4] After just ten months, Walt sold the paper and obtained a job working as a typesetter for the *Long Island Democrat*. While there he wrote a series of articles entitled *The Sun-Down Papers*. Leaving that position, he again returned to teaching but moved continually from job to job. Later he wrote, "O, damnation, damnation! Thy other name is school-teaching."[5]

From the years of 1841 through 1848, Whitman's jobs were varied, but they all involved journalism. He worked as a printer, writer, and editor. Walt's residences were varied, too, living in many boarding houses in Long Island and Brooklyn. In 1842, he wrote his first novel, *Franklin Evans* or *The Inebriate Novel*. This piece of temperance fiction, in which he promoted prohibition, sold 20,000 copies, more than anything Whitman ever sold in his life.

The first part of 1848, Walt was offered a position in Mississippi. He received $200 for travel expenses and was accompanied by his fifteen year old brother, Jeff. They left New York by train and went to Baltimore. From there they traveled by train, stagecoach, and boat to New Orleans. The trip on a Mississippi steamer later inspired Walt's poem, "The Mississippi at Midnight." Walt worked for the *New Orleans Daily Crescent* doing office work and delivery. He usually wrote articles on current events but avoided writing about politics. Walt was an avid observer. Here he noticed the stark differences between his rural Long Island and bustling, colorful New Orleans. Here it was common to see sailors, streetwalkers, vendors, shopkeepers, and actors intermingling. He witnessed the horrors of slaves being sold on the street. Walt visited markets, bars, and theaters and saw a city which was a melting pot of different races and nationalities. Jeff became ill and homesick, so the brothers returned to Brooklyn within a year.

In all of his travels, Walt carried in his pocket tiny, homemade notebooks which were essentially pieces of paper tied together with ribbon or pin. Whenever he saw, felt, or heard something that he wanted to remember he would immediately jot it down. These notes later spawned writings or poems.

At the time this photograph was taken, Walt owned a print shop.

Walt returned home during the election year of 1848 and immediately got involved in politics. In August, he attended, as a delegate, a nominating convention of the Free-Soil Party which believed that slavery should not extend into the western territories. While at the convention he heard such orators as Frederick Douglas. Inspired by the gathering, he founded a newspaper, the *Brooklyn Freeman*. The Free-Soil Party's candidate, Martin Van Buren, lost to Zachary Taylor, but Walt continued to run the paper for around a year.

From 1850 through 1854, Whitman owned his own print shop and stationery store. He was a voracious writer and submitted political poems to various newspapers, many of them being dark, angry, and rebellious. During this time he also became a real estate speculator and attempted to emulate his father's previous business of building and selling houses. At first he did well, but later this career failed. His brother George, who worked with him, later recalled, "There was a great boom in Brooklyn in the early fifties, and he had his chance then, but you know he made nothing of that chance."[6]

This engraving was used as the frontispiece in Walt's first edition of *Leaves of Grass*.

In 1855, Walt's *Leaves of Grass* was printed by the Rome Brothers in Brooklyn. These two Scottish immigrants lived in his neighborhood. Therefore, Walt was right there during the printing process. He said, "I always superintended, and sometimes undertook part of the work myself, as I am a printer and can use the 'stick,' you know."[7] The book was very small as Whitman wanted people to be able to stick it in their pockets. It consisted of 95 pages and twelve untitled poems. Curiously, it did not display Whitman's name, but it displayed his picture. The title was thought to be journalist jargon. "Grass" was what publishers called work of minor value and "leaves" was another name for pages.

The book contained a new style of poetry, not the rhyming verse to which many Americans were accustomed. A few poems alluded to the human body and senses. Some critics considered Whitman's poems fresh and new, while others considered them vulgar, coarse, and lewd. Poems, which were later named "Song of Myself" and "I Sing the Body Electric," introduced readers to the atrocities of slavery. Therefore, *Leaves of Grass* was praised by African-Americans. Sojourner Truth heard a person reading from the book and asked who wrote it. Then she said, "Never mind the man's name - it was God who wrote it, he chose the man - to give his message."[8] Walt wanted his words to appeal to all Americas regardless of race, occupation, age, or status.

Walt sent a copy of his new book to Ralph Waldo Emerson, because Emerson had written an essay in 1844 expressing the need for America to have its own poet who would speak about the uniqueness of the United States and its people.

Emerson wrote a letter to Walt stating that the book was "the most extraordinary piece of wit and wisdom America has yet contributed." He also wrote he was greeting him "at the beginning of a great career."[9]

Shortly thereafter, Emerson met with Southern abolitionist Moncure Daniel Conway. (Conway was born in Stafford and lived in his Falmouth house on River Road until he went away to college.) The poet suggested Conway read *Leaves of Grass*. He did so and wished to meet the author. Traveling to New York by steamer, he stopped at the Whitman home. His mother said that her son was at the Rome Printing Office, so Conway found him there revising a proof. Conway wrote a letter to Emerson describing Walt's appearance:

> A man you would not have marked in a thousand; blue striped shirt, opening from a red throat; and sitting on a chair without a back, which, being the only one, he offered me, and sat down on a round of the printer's desk himself. His manner was blunt enough also, without being disagreeably so . . . The likeness in the book is fair. His beard and hair are greyer than is usual with a man of thirty-six. His face and eye are interesting, and his head rather narrow behind the eyes; but a thick brow looks as if it might have absorbed much.[10]

After discussing Emerson and *Leaves of Grass*, Walt accompanied Conway on a ferry into town. Conway thought Whitman was a "hail fellow" with every man he met, most of whom were the working class. Conway's letter continues:

> He says he is one of that class by choice; that he is personally dear to some thousands of such in New York, who 'love him but cannot make head or tail of his book.' He rides on the stage with the driver. Stops to talk with the old man or woman selling fruit at the street corner. And his dress, etc., is consistent with that.

Conway concluded the letter by saying of Walt, "He is clearly his Book."[11]

Around the time *Leaves of Grass* was published, Walt became disgusted with politics and the various parties. He wrote perceptively that political parties consisted of, "empty flesh, putrid mouths, mumbling and squeaking the tones of these conventions, the politicians standing back in the shadow, telling lies."[12] Biographer Reynolds wrote, "In 1855 Whitman believed that the United States, cut adrift from its

Moncure Daniel Conway, a Southern abolitionist and Stafford native, first met Walt in 1855.

original ideals, desperately needed poets."[13] Walt decided to free himself from any party and work on editing portions of *Leaves of Grass*. In July of that year, Walt's father passed away.

Just a year later, in 1856, Walt wrote a second edition of *Leaves of Grass* which was expanded to 384 pages and contained thirty-two titled poems. It was much thicker and had a green cover with a gold-leafed title along with the author's name. Costing just a dollar, this beautiful publication looked much more like a true volume of poetry. In the back was a collection of letters Whitman received, including Emerson's. However, Walt did not get Emerson's approval for its inclusion. He also included his own response to Emerson's letter. After discovering this, Emerson confided in Conway that if he had known his letter would be published he might have qualified his praise. "There are parts of the book," he said "where I hold my nose as I read."[14]

During the summer, Conway decided to visit Walt again. This time Conway was staying at the Metropolitan Hotel along with his sister. Before he left to see Walt, he read some passages of Walt's book to his sister and his sister's friend. They enjoyed the verse and requested that he ask Walt to join them for dinner. In his autobiography, Conway wrote:

> . . . he came in baize coat and chequered shirt, in fact just like the portrait in his book. The ladies were pleased with him; his manners were good, and his talk entertaining. Walt Whitman told me that I was the first who had visited him because of his book.[15]

Conway also later recalled a 1857 visit with Walt:

> . . . I found him at the top of a hill near by lying on his back and gazing on the sky . . . We first went to his house, where I talked a few moments with his mother, a plain pleasant old lady not so grey as her son, and whose dark eyes had an apprehensive look. It was a small frame house. He took me to his little room with its cot, and poor furniture . . . There were no books in the room, and he told me he had very few, but had the use of good libraries . . . We passed the day 'loafing' on Staten Island, where we found groves and solitary beaches now built over. We had a good long bath in the sea, and I perceived that the reddish tanned face and neck of the poet crowned a body of lily-like whiteness and a shapely form.[16]

Walt became the editor of the *Brooklyn Times* for two years, from 1857-1859. Then he was out of work during the winter of the next year. This was called his "Bohemian phase" where he frequented such places as the underground restaurant, Pfaff's, a gathering place for New York's Bohemian culture including theatrical and literary types.

Walt Whitman

This picture was taken when Walt was
in his "Bohemian phase" of life.

In 1860, Walt's life became more focused when a third edition of *Leaves of Grass* was published in Boston. This time the book consisted of 456 pages and was bound in orange cloth. It had symbols on the front of a rising sun and a butterfly perched on a hand. The publishers subsequently went broke, and Walt only received $250.

Whitman always remembered the start of the Civil War in April of 1861. He had just watched a performance of Verdi's *A Masked Ball* and was walking down Broadway when he heard newsboys shout that Fort Sumter had been attacked.

After the start of the war, Walt wrote poems such as, "Beat! Beat! Drums!" that encouraged patriotism and attempted to rally the North. Walt also contributed many articles for newspapers which were signed "Velsor Brush." Velsor was his mother's maiden name and Brush was the maiden name of his grandmother.[17] Articles, using that pseudonym, written about Broadway Hospital, praised the facility for using the newest methods of surgery for the Civil War wounded. We know the articles were written by Walt, as he often volunteered at that hospital, and there was a direct correlation between the words written in his pocket-sized hospital notebooks and those used in the articles.

Walt was already familiar with the sorrow of war by witnessing the wounded at the hospital, so one can imagine the angst he felt when reading that his brother George had been injured during the Battle of Fredericksburg. On Tuesday, December 16th, within two hours of reading the notice, he threw some notebooks and clothes into a carpetbag and withdrew fifty dollars from his mother's bank account.[18] Walt was quickly on his way to Virginia.

George Washington Whitman,
Walt's brother, served in Stafford.

While changing cars in Philadelphia, Walt had his pocket picked, so he ended up in Washington, D.C. without a dime. In a letter to his mother he tells about his harrowing adventures:

> The next two days I spent hunting through the hospitals, walking day and night, unable to ride, trying to get information – trying to get access to big people, etc. – I could not get the least clue to anything . . . But Thursday afternoon, I lit on a way to get down on the Government boat that runs to Aquia creek, and so by railroad to the neighborhood of Falmouth, opposite Fredericksburg – so by degrees I worked my way to Ferrero's brigade, which I found Friday afternoon without much trouble after I got in camp. When I found dear brother George, and found that he was alive and well, O you may imagine how trifling all my little cares and difficulties seemed – they vanished into nothing.[19]

We know the exact extent of the wound that George received, as he had written a letter home on December 16, 1862. Ironically, that was the same date that the New York newspaper had published the article about his wound. In the letter George wrote, "Dear Mother, We have had another battle and I have come out safe and sound, although I had the side of my jaw slightly scraped with a peice [sic] of shell which burst at my feet."[20]

Whitman's notes taken while in Falmouth speak volumes. The following notes were written after his visit to the Lacy House:

> . . . at the foot of tree, immediately in front, a heap of feet, legs, arms, and human fragments, cut, bloody, black and blue, swelled and sickening – in the garden near, a row of graves; some distance back, a little while afterwards, I saw a long row of them.[21]

> The large mansion is quite crowded, upstairs and down, everything impromptu, no system, all bad enough, but I have no doubt the best that can be done; all the wounds pretty bad, some frightful, the men in their old clothes, unclean and bloody. Some of the wounded are rebel soldiers and officers, prisoners . . . I went through the rooms, downstairs and up. Some of the men were dying. I had nothing to give at that visit, but wrote a few letters to folks home, mothers, &c.[22]

His notes also describe the sight from Falmouth looking at devastated Fredericksburg:

> The walk along the Rappahannock in front, a pleasant shore, with trees –
> See that old town over there – how splintered, bursted, crumbled, the houses –
> some with their chimneys thrown down . . .[23]

Evidently, Walt also went over to Fredericksburg. He did not write it in his notes, but did in a letter to two friends. " – have gone over with a flag of truce the next day to help direct the burial of the dead –"[24] This probably did happen, as a *New York Herald* article mentioned that a flag of truce was sent to the Confederate headquarters in Fredericksburg to ask permission to bury the dead, as the battlefield was thickly covered with the unburied.[25]

On Sunday night, December 21th, Walt walked around George's camp. (George's 51st New York Infantry was in Ferrero's brigade in the 2nd Division, IX Army Corps.) Fires were burning and "playing light on the faces." He sat down and listened while they sang "merry song." Yet, among the merriment, the group would discuss the death of some of their fallen comrades.

The next day Walt wrote about witnessing a balloon launch near The Phillips House.

> Monday, Dec. 22 – forenoon very pleasant. Sun shining, a partial haze – Saw the balloon up – a great huge, slow moving thing, with a curious look to me, as it crawled up, and slanted down again, as if it were alive. The haze, I suppose, prevented any good use – for it staid up only a little while. A beautiful object to me – a graceful, pear-shaped thing, some 30 by 50 feet, (at a guess.) I examined it, by and by, when it was grappled on the ground, in a picturesque ravine, west of Gen. Sumner's headquarters, swelling up there in its diamond-shaped netting, with a watchful sentry over it night and day.[26] (Walt, like others, continued to refer to The Phillips House as Sumner's headquarters when, in actuality, it was the headquarters of Burnside.)

On Tuesday, Walt was on the hill by The Phillips House and looked down at the Falmouth Railroad Station (which is today's location of the Fraternal Order of Eagles Lodge on Cool Spring Road) and described the scene:

> The day is soft, brightly beautiful. Down below is spread out a picturesque scene. The countless baggage wagons, with their white roofs, the numerous strings of mules, the railroad locomotive, the broad spread of slopes and hills winding their way over the railroad track, and making a huge S. towards the river, which is only a few hundred yards distant, are the whole of the 51st N.Y. 51st Penn. And 100 men of the 11th N.H. going on picket duty along the shore.[27]

This postwar etching, showing Whitman as the third man in the chow line, was done by Civil War artist Edwin Forbes and based on his wartime Stafford sketches.

Whitman continued visiting camps in Falmouth and around the Lacy House. On Friday morning he witnessed a sight he would never forget.

> Early this morning I walked out, in the open fields, one side of the camp. I found some of the soldiers digging graves – they were for the 51st N.Y. and 11th N.H. There was a row of graves there already, each with a slat or a board, generally a piece of barrelhead, on which was inscribed the name of the soldier. Death is nothing here. As you step out in the morning from your tent to wash your face you see before you on a stretcher a shapeless extended object, and over it is thrown a dark grey blanket – it is the corpse of some wounded or sick soldier of the reg't who died in the hospital tent during the night – perhaps there is a row of three or four of these corpses lying covered over. No one makes an ado. There is a detail of men made to bury them; all useless ceremony is omitted.[28]

Walt also described the barren land of war-devastated Stafford. Endless supplies of trees were needed to help shelter the 135,000 Union troops, keep them warm, cook their food, and create their bridges and corduroy roads.

> I walked on over to a camp of teamsters, in the woods – or rather what had been the woods, but was now pretty well cut down; a few trees standing at intervals, stumps all over and plenty of boughs and branches strewing the ground. The teamsters were in groups around, there and there, mostly squatted – by the fires, idling, or cooking breakfast, &c.[29]

On December 25th Walt spends some time in Falmouth contemplating. He wrote:

> I hear plainly the music of a good band, at some Brigadier's quarters, a mile and a half away; it is a beautiful soft sunny Christmas day with thin haze in the air. Then the drum tap from one direction or other comes constantly breaking in. Where I sit, I am not within many hundred rods of any soldiers' quarters, but I can see them, regiments, brigades and divisions, spread out in the distance, at every point of the compass. All is open ground; not a particle of fence anywhere... but where I sit a couple of hundred feet off a road, I am quite solitary. I hear the sound of bugle calls, very martial, at this distance – a fine large troop of cavalry is just passing, the hoofs of the horses shake the ground, and I hear the clatter of sabers. Amid all this pleasant scene, under the sweet sky and warm sun, I sit and think over the battle of last Saturday week.[30]

Whitman's observations about the Union troops were, at times, quite poignant.

> The mass of our men in our army are young – it is an impressive sight to me to see the countless numbers of youths and boys – there is only a sprinkling of elderly men. On a parade at evening, there you see them, - poor lads, many of them already with the experiences of the oldest veterans.[31]

Years later, in 1881, Walt recounted some of his Falmouth experiences when he wrote the poem the "Wound Dresser."

> *Bearing the bandages, water and sponge,*
> *Straight and swift to my wounded I go,*
> *Where they lie on the ground after the battle brought in,*
> *Where their priceless blood reddens the grass the ground . . .*[32]

Walt returned to Washington and aided wounded soldiers. The U.S. Capitol dome was not yet completed.

After two weeks in the Stafford area and volunteering wherever he could, Walt traveled to Washington D.C. on January 2nd. He felt his nursing would be of greater value in the hospitals located in the nation's capital, as over 9,000 wounded had been evacuated there. He obtained part-time work at the army paymaster's office enabling him to travel to hospitals during off-hours. He wrote of his experiences in an article, "The Great Army of the Sick" for a New York newspaper.

For years, Walt served long hours in Washington, D.C.'s Civil War hospitals.

There were many letters that Walt wrote to family members and friends during his time in Washington. The Whitmans were a very closely knit family. If George sent a letter to his mother, she might send it to Walt. Walt, in turn, would send it to another member of the family.

The fall and winter of 1864 was not a happy period for Walt, as his brother George was captured by the Confederates the end of September. *The New York Times* printed an article about George's volunteer infantry on October 29, 1864 which was called, "Fifty-First New York City Veterans." Although no authorship was attributed to the piece, it was probably written by Walt, as it included passages from his notes and portions of letters that George had sent family members.

George's capture greatly affected Walt. He reflected:

> He had now to endure that worst part of a soldier's experience of life – if that
> can be called life, which is worse than death – in one after another of the
> Confederates States military prisons; a series of many weary months of starvation,
> humiliation, and every pressure on body and spirit, of which the world knows
> too well.[33]

In 1864, Whitman worked as a clerk for the Department of the Interior.

In December, his brother Andrew Jackson Whitman died due to tuberculosis complicated by the effects of alcoholism. Later that month, Walt had to commit his brother Jesse to a lunatic asylum. His insanity was attributed to a fall from a ship years earlier.

The start of 1864 brought better times for Whitman as he was appointed a clerk in the Bureau of Indian Affairs in the Department of the Interior. His yearly salary was $1,200. He worked in the office with Indians to "negotiate for supplies, annuities, and treaty lands."[34] Much to Walt's relief, George was released from imprisonment in February.

Whitman happened to be out of town on April 14, 1865, when Abraham Lincoln was assassinated. It affected him deeply, as he had truly loved Lincoln. He never met him in person but had probably seen him around town twenty to thirty times. "I see the President almost every day," he had written in 1863. Sometimes Lincoln was on a gray horse and was escorted by twenty cavalrymen in yellow-striped jackets or else would be riding in a carriage with his wife. Walt wrote, "We have got so that we exchange bows, and very cordial ones." He also wrote, "He has a face like a hoosier Michel Angelo [sic], so awful ugly it becomes beautiful, with its strange mouth, its deep cut, criss-cross lines, and its doughnut complexion."[35] Ironically, Walt never knew that Lincoln had read *Leaves of Grass*. In 1916, Henry Rankin wrote in *Personal Reflections of Abraham Lincoln* that in 1857, Lincoln picked up a copy of his book in his Springfield law office and was so impressed by it that he read it aloud to his colleagues.

In June of 1865, Walt was fired from his job, as someone noticed a copy of *Leaves of Grass* on his desk which was marked with his editorial comments. Since this book was considered indecent by James Harlan, Secretary of the Interior, Walt was removed from his office, as it was felt he might injure the morals of the department. Regardless, Walt was able to gain a transfer to the Attorney General's office in July. Whitman's friend, William Douglas O'Connor, was incensed when he heard about the firing and in January of 1866 published a pamphlet entitled, *The Good Gray Poet*. It emphasized Walt's wartime patriotism. This publication helped increase Whitman's celebrity and popularity.

Walt continued volunteering in the last remaining Civil War hospital in D.C., Harewood, until it closed in April of 1866. He estimated that throughout the years he helped between 80,000 to 100,000 wounded and ill. In his small, homemade notebooks he had jotted down soldiers names, wounds or illnesses, and any treat they wanted like apples, oranges, sponge cake, or horehound candy. For years, he tried to fulfill their desires.

In the fall of 1866, Walt took leave in order to prepare for yet another publication of *Leaves of Grass*. He had difficulty finding a publisher, and it was not published until the following year. Walt said that this 1867 edition was "a new & much better edition of *Leaves of Grass* complete – that *unkillable* work!"[36] He thought this would be the last publication and even omitted his photo.

In 1868, *Poems of Walt Whitman* was published in England. Moncure Daniel Conway, who was now living in England, acted as literary agent and assisted W.M. Rossetti of London in its publication. All of a sudden, Walt obtained international recognition. Moncure Conway received a letter from Walt dated February 17th. He told of his joy in being accepted abroad.

> Indeed, my dear friend, I may here confess to you that to be accepted by those young men of England, & so treated with highest courtesy & even honor, touches me deeply. In my own country, so far, from the organs, the press, & from authoritative sources, I have received but one long tirade of shallow impudence, mockery, and scurrilous jeers. Only since the English recognition have the skies here lifted up a little.

In 1869 Whitman's work was selling well abroad.

In Walt's letter he told Conway that, "I remain well & hearty – occupy the same quite agreeable & quiet berth in the Attorney General's office – and, at leisure, am writing a prose piece or two. (which I will send you when printed.)"[37]

The year of 1871 brought forth still another edition of *Leaves of Grass*. However, unlike the previous edition, this volume contained several photographs of the poet. In 1872, he quit his job and traveled home to care for his elderly mother who was battling arthritis. A year later, Walt had a stroke leaving him paralyzed on his left side. Five months later, his mother passed away. Wanting to leave sorrow behind, he moved to Camden, New Jersey, where he lived with his brother George until he was able to buy his own house on Mickle Street in 1884.

Whitman spent the last years of his life on Mickle Street in Camden, New Jersey.

Walt lived on Mickle Street for eight years, six of which were with Mary Oakes Davis, a sea captain's widow. She obtained free room and board for housekeeping duties. Walt had little furniture, so he asked her to bring her pieces to fill out his home. Mary also brought quite a menagerie with her: a cat, a dog, two turtle-doves, a canary, a robin and hens for the exterior.[38] The dog soon became the bane of Walt's existence. He said, "He is the nastiest, noisiest, silliest, stupidest, horriblest dog that was ever born – a pest, a continual sore in my side!"[39]

In 1886 and 1887 Walt gave talks about Lincoln around the country. He was finally receiving some notoriety and fame, but a year later Walt was no longer vigorous. Physically, he was feeling very weak.

Amazingly, there were further editions of *Leaves of Grass*, in 1876, 1881, and 1889. The last edition came in 1891. Walt wrote a friend, "L. of G. at last complete – after 33 y'rs of hackling at it, all times & moods of my life, fair weather & foul, all parts of the land, and peace & war, young and old."[40] This latest volume contained 400 poems, a marked contrast to the first volume of twelve poems. The picture of Whitman featured in that book showed an older poet with a white flowing beard. This edition has been called the "Deathbed Edition," as he was planning for his death. He had a large granite tomb shaped like a home constructed for $4,000.

Toward the end of his life, Walt was in constant pain and had difficulty breathing. This was aggravated by "half-paralysis" from strokes in 1888. Whitman's room was quite large and very simple. Two portraits of his parents were the only decorations. His small bed rested on plank flooring Three windows faced the street, but he kept them shuttered much of the time to make the room rather dark. The room, itself, was cluttered with his books, newspapers, articles, manuscripts, and correspondence. He became agitated when Mrs. Davis tried to organize his belongings. When he felt like working, he would sit in a large rocking chair and write using a quill pen with a pad on his knee.

Whitman never wanted his cluttered room organized.
He typically wrote in his rocking chair with a pad on his knee.

Whitman died on March 26, 1892 at his Camden home. The official cause of death was, "pleurisy of the left side, consumption of the right lung, general miliary tuberculosis and parenchymatous nephritis."[41] Three days later his body was on display for viewing, and thousands of people trampled through his simple house for three hours. Flowers and wreaths from all over the world overflowed the oak coffin and surrounding area. A carriage took Whitman's body two miles down the road to Harleigh Cemetery where nearly four thousand people paid tribute to America's poet. Bands played, speeches were given by friends, and refreshments were served. It was said that Whitman's funeral was "wholly without parallel in America."[42] John Burroughs, Whitman's friend and first biographer wrote, "When I saw the crowds of common people that flocked to Walt Whitman's funeral, I said, How fit, how touching all this is; how well it would please him . . .[43]"

Dr. Mary Edwards Walker

A Woman Doctor in Pants

*W*hereas Clara Barton has been described as an angel or humanitarian, Dr. Mary Walker has been called unconventional, eccentric, and a "sideshow freak."[1] Mary's non-conformity apparently was encouraged as a small child from her parents. She was born on November 26, 1832, to Alvah and Vesta Walker on a farm in Oswego, New York. She was the fifth daughter born to the couple. Mary's parents gave very unique names to some of their daughters, like Luna and Aurora Borealis. A brother was born later increasing the family to eight. Believing in a popular loose-clothing movement, Mary's father convinced his daughters that wearing restrictive corsets was unhealthy. The belief was contrary to the style of most young ladies during this and the approaching Victorian era. Mary's parents also believed that all their children should be educated, not just their son. So Mary attended a common school which was built on land her father contributed to Oswego in 1833. It was known as school #15.

After common school and graduation from Falley Seminary in Fulton, New York, Mary taught school for a while just like her sisters. At twenty-one years of age, she entered the Syracuse Medical School. After three, thirteen-week classes, she graduated with honors, the first woman from that school and only the second woman in the U.S. to obtain a medical degree. However, that did not guarantee success, for after practicing medicine for several months in Columbus, Ohio, she returned to New York and married a fellow medical school classmate, Albert Miller. The wedding was quite unique as the bride wore bloomers. Bloomers were pants named after Amelia Jenks Bloomer and were popular in the early 1850s. The pants were baggy and gathered around the ankle. Over the bloomers. Mary wore a knee-length shirt or dress coat. She insisted that the wedding ceremony not include a promise to "obey." She noted, "How barbarous the very idea of one equal promising to be the slave of another . . ."[2] She also did not take her husband's name, but instead used it as a middle name. Therefore, she was known as Dr. Mary Edwards Miller Walker.

The newlyweds opened up a practice together. Unfortunately, the marriage lasted just a short time due to her husband's unfaithfulness. It took Mary ten years to actually get a legal divorce. In doing so, she became the first woman in New York to be granted a divorce on the grounds of infidelity. After getting the official decree, she wrote across the document "Divorce – Last of the Villain."[3]

After separating from her husband, Mary set up a practice above a Rome, New York haberdashery. Her practice was small, enabling her time to advocate for dress reform and to contribute articles for a newspaper, *Sybil*. Dr. Walker believed that a corset was "a coffin contrived of steel bands." She also argued that bloomers were less cumbersome and healthier than "normal" women's clothing and felt it more "physiological."[4]

With the outbreak of the Civil War in 1861, Mary closed her practice in Rome and traveled to Washington, D.C. where she applied to the War Department for a surgeon's commission in the Union Army. Knowing full well that the Union needed surgeons, she was hopeful of obtaining a commission. However, the Surgeon General turned her down because of regulations and the tradition of never before having a woman in that capacity. Additionally, because it was unprecedented, no thought had been given to commissioning women in any capacity.

This photograph of Mary Walker is one of the earliest that exists.

Undaunted, Mary remained in Washington, D.C. as an unpaid volunteer in army hospitals. Most of her time was spent with the soldiers from Indiana who were housed at the U.S. Patent Office. Dr. J.N. Green was in charge of the hospital and lacked an assistant, so Mary took over the position. She so impressed Dr. Green that he wrote a letter recommending her for a paid appointment. The letter, which Mary gave to the Surgeon General, stated, "If there is any way of securing to her compensation, you would confer a favor by lending her your influence."[5] The letter fell of deaf ears, so Dr. Green attempted to give Mary money from his own salary, but she declined saying he had a family while she did not. The entire time she was at the Patent Office she bedded down in the hospital alcove and ate the same rations given the patients. Later, she moved to Forest Hall Prison in Georgetown and cared for more wounded.

Taking some time off in January of 1862, Mary traveled back to New York. In March she took classes at Hygeia Therapeutic College in the city. The school emphasized "natural" cures and stressed good hygiene. In a short time she obtained additional certificates and returned to her home in Oswego to begin lecturing. In the fall, Mary returned to Washington, D.C. Shortly thereafter, she left the district and traveled to Warrenton, Virginia where Major General Ambrose Burnside and the Army of the Potomac were headquartered. Again she requested to be commissioned but was rejected. She volunteered her services again in tent hospitals. Sometime during this period, Mary started wearing the uniform of a Union Army officer. Records do not indicate anyone giving her permission to do so, but her garb consisted of gold-striped trousers and a green surgeon's sash. A felt hat with gold cord sat upon the head of this petite, five foot woman.

While in Warrenton, Mary realized that some of the wounded needed to be taken to D.C. for better care and adequate medical supplies. Convincing Burnside that this would be best for the men, he wrote the following:

> The General Commanding directs that Dr. Mary E. Walker be authorized to accompany and assist in caring for, from Warrenton Virginia to Washington D.C., the sick and wounded soldiers now at the former post. The Surgeon in Charge there will afford every facility to Dr. Walker for that purpose. Dr. Walker is entitled to transportation to Washington . . .[6]

After delivering the patients by train, Mary discovered that Burnside was marching to Falmouth. In December of 1862, she found out about the disastrous outcome for the Union forces during the Battle of Fredericksburg. Still without official standing, Mary immediately traveled to Stafford where she again offered assistance. Letters indicate Mary worked there in tent hospitals and was also at the Lacy House. A *New York Tribune* article refers to Dr. Walker at the Lacy House but describes her apparel as slightly different from that in Warrenton. It also has her working with the Sanitation Commission:

> Among the unmarshalled [sic] host of camp-followers of the old army, not the least noteworthy personage is Miss Mary E. Walker, or "Dr. Walker" as she is usually styled . . . She is a native of New York, has received a regular medical education, and believes her sex ought not to disqualify her for the performance of deeds of mercy to the suffering heroes of the Republic. Dressed in male habiliments, with the exception of a girlish-looking straw hat, decked off with an ostrich feather, with a petite figure and feminine features, the tout ensemble is quite engaging a jaunty air of dignity well calculated to receive the sincere respect of the soldiers . . . She can amputate a limb with the skill of an old surgeon, and administer medicine equally as well. Strange to say that, although she had frequently applied for a permanent position in the medical corps, she has never been formally assigned to any particular duty . . . She is at present temporarily attached to the Sanitation Commission, whose headquarters are at the Lacey [sic] opposite Fredericksburg. We will add that the lady referred to is exceedingly popular among the soldiers in the hospitals, and is undoubtedly doing much good.[7]

Later in life, Mary wrote only three distinct remembrances of her time in Stafford:

> At one time, when I was down to the Lacy House at Fredericksburg, after the famous battle there. When the wounded were brought from Fredericksburg to near this house, I was directed by the managing surgeons to take any cases I chose and dress them preparatory to sending them to Washington. Among these cases was a man where a shell had taken a part of his skull away, about as large a piece as a dollar, although not the same shape. I could see the pulsation of the brain, and when he talked I could see a movement of the same, slight though it was. He was perfectly sensible, and although I never saw him after he was taken to Washington, I learned that he lived several days.[8]

Aquia Landing became a busy port, evacuating injured soldiers to Washington, D.C.

Mary also recalled when wounded men were being taken out on stretchers and set down on the bank of the Potomac River awaiting a boat to arrive at Aquia Landing from Washington. Standing by the edge of the water, she noticed the wounded were carried headfirst across a "gangway" into the vessel. She directed them to be immediately turned around and taken feet first. She wrote:

> It is almost needless to say that men who were wounded so that they were obliged to be taken on stretchers and very ill so that they could not walk, taking them down head first would have produced pains in the head if not serious congestion of the brain on such a warm day. I was wearing my green surgeon's sash although I had not then any government authority to do so.[9]

Mary's compassion was shown in her writings about a young Union drummer boy who "had been wounded so severely in both legs" that they had to be amputated. Behind enemy lines in Fredericksburg, Confederate surgeons performed the operation. There was an exchange of prisoners, so the young man was shipped to Washington D.C. from Stafford. Mary discovered that the young boy was from New York and the only child of a widow. He was taken to Armory Square Hospital where he passed away a day or two after his arrival.

> A few days after this I found a man [woman] in great distress regarding her failure to find her son, who was a drummer boy, and whom through some source she had learned had lost his legs by an explosion of a shell. The description of her son, the times and place where she had last learned of him, and its being the only case similar at the battle of Fredericksburg, I was convinced, after investigation, was her son. I can never forget the agonized expression of that woman's face. I did her some little favors that were in my power to do; and as she stated she could not go back to her home as her boy was gone, and that she desired to do what she could for other mother's sons. Through an effort of mine a place was secured for her as a nurse in the insane asylum in Washington where a number of soldiers had been sent, who from wounds, sickness and other causes had lost the proper use of their mental faculties.[10]

While back in D.C., Walker helped the wounded again. But while there, she discovered many women had difficulty finding their loved ones in hospitals. In some cases it took days for them to find their relatives. Considering that a woman of that time "should never travel alone," these "searching women" had difficulties finding lodging and food. Seeing a need, Mary wrote to the mayor and asked for help in finding a house which could be used for temporary lodging. Needing money to rent a house, Mary gave speeches to raise available funds. Finding a house across the street from Ford's Theatre, she went to General Edward Canby

and subsequently asked for any furniture, sheets, bed linens, and blankets he might be able to donate. Once the house was up and running, Mary started helping the women find their relatives, because wounded were scattered in hospitals all around Washington, Alexandria, and Georgetown. She even asked General Daniel Rucker to have an ambulance and driver report to her daily so that the searches would become easier. Walker eventually formed an association which helped these women in need, but she later turned the association over to some physicians' wives.

Daniel H. Rucker helped both
Mary Walker and Clara Barton.

The fall of 1863 found Mary in Chattanooga, Tennessee, where she was chosen to be assistant surgeon to the 52nd Ohio Infantry. There she wore her "modified" uniform but also included two pistols which she wore constantly. Major General George H. Thomas requested her abilities, as the regiment's previous doctor had passed away. Mary worked with Major General Alexander McCook who greatly appreciated her. But other doctors strenuously objected. A Dr. Perin, who was the medical director of the Army of the Cumberland, ordered her examined. A committee of five doctors determined it was "doubtful whether she has pursued the study of medicine." They felt that her expertise was "not much greater than most housewives."[11] But since there was a shortage of doctors, Mary remained working with a grateful McCook in spite of the committee's damning report.

Later that year, and into 1864, Mary attempted to help Confederate civilians. She had heard that they were suffering from malnourishment and disease due to lack of medical supplies. Traveling behind enemy lines, with approval from Major General McCook, she was frequently stopped in her Union "uniform." Once the Southerners realized that she was actually saving lives, she was allowed to pass. It was during this time that Mary wrote President Abraham Lincoln asking for a commission. Five days later, she received his reply written upon her letter. He rejected her request.

However, Mary continued trying to help Confederate civilians. In the spring, while she was in Georgia, near the border with Tennessee, Mary was captured by a sentry and taken to Confederate General Johnston. She was then sent by train to Richmond where she would be placed in a prison called Castle Thunder.

News of the "captured woman-oddity" was telegraphed along rail lines, so that crowds congregated at railroad stations to see this "spy." One of the gawkers in Richmond was Captain Joseph Semmes who wrote his wife a letter stating, "[We] were all amused and disgusted . . . at the sight of a thing that nothing but the debased and depraved Yankee nation could produce . . . she was . . . not good looking and of course had tongue enough for a regiment of men . . . she would be more at home in a lunatic asylum."[12]

Mary was imprisoned in Castle Thunder, a converted Richmond tobacco factory.

Newspapers reported Mary had fights with roommates while in prison.

While being a prisoner of war, Mary wrote her parents so they would not worry:

> I hope you are not grieving about me . . . I am living in a three-story brick 'castle' with plenty to eat, and a clean bed to sleep in . . . the officers are gentlemanly and kind, and it will not be long before I am exchanged.[13]

The letter she had written could not have been further from the truth, for her bed was infected with fleas and bedbugs, and rats roamed her room at night. Her food consisted of maggot-filled rice and moldy bread. Complaining to authorities, Mary finally got the Confederates to add wheat bread and cabbage to daily rations. Despite such changes, Mary wrote that she weighed only 60 lbs. when she left the castle. Her weight upon entering was 105 lbs. She also declared that her eyesight was failing due to her imprisonment.

A *Richmond Examiner* newspaper article, dated June 29, 1864, does not reflect Mary's frailty, in fact quite the opposite:

Miss Walker, the Yankee Surgeoness

Miss Doctress, Miscegenation, Philosophical Walker, who has so long ensconced herself very quietly in Castle Thunder, has loomed into activity again. Recently she got mad, pitched into several of her room-mates in long clothes, and tore out handfuls of auburn hair from the head of one of them. Then she proclaimed succession, and went into another apartment, where she is now lady and lioness of all she surveys. Sometimes she exhibits herself in costume on the balcony of the Castle, or walks in the garden below by permission of the urbane commandant of the post . . . Her miscegenation suit is getting rusty, and she thinks it hard, very hard, that she is not allowed to go home.

After being there for four months, Walker was freed along with several hundred prisoners. They were taken by boat to Fortress Monroe in Virginia. Mary was pleased that she was exchanged for a six-foot Confederate major, for she felt this tended to legitimatize her military status.

Walker returned to the 52nd Ohio to retrieve her belongings. While there, she wrote to Major General William Tecumseh Sherman asking for pay and the rank of major, the rank of a regimental surgeon assistant. She was supported in her request by Major General Thomas. The previous order by Major General McCook, saying she was assigned as assistant surgeon to the Fifty-Second Ohio, accompanied the request. Secretary of War Edwin Stanton approved the request and in September of 1864, Mary received $432.36 pay for being an assistant surgeon. In three years this was the first time she was actually paid for her service to the country. Unfortunately, she was again denied a commission.

Afterwards, in the fall of 1864, Mary was assigned as "surgeon in charge" of the Louisville Female Military Prison which held Confederate women. For this she would be given a little over $100 a month for working as a contracted civilian, not as an Army surgeon. Mary had some conflicts with a doctor who previously held her position. She tried to make needed changes but requested a transfer after six months. She then held a position in Clarksville, Tennessee at a refugee home and orphans' asylum. She stayed there until the Civil War was over in April of 1865 following General Lee's surrender at Appomattox.

Walker returned to Washington after the war. She had always wished to resume her private practice, but she did not think she was able due to damaged eyesight. So, she started to apply for positions such as the medical inspector at the Bureau of Refugees, Freedmen and Abandoned Lands. She even tried to obtain a postwar commission. Mary boldly sent her list of accomplishments to then President Andrew Johnson. Accompanying her application were character references from her friends. Johnson was impressed, but forwarded the requests to others, and Mary was rejected again. But in November of 1865, President Johnson and two of Mary's closest allies, Major General Sherman and Major General Thomas, wished to recognize her for all her service to the country. She was awarded the Congressional Medal of Honor for meritorious service, being the first woman to ever receive this award. She felt she finally obtained approbation for all that she had done.

Mary was proud of receiving the Medal of Honor. She wore it constantly.

Her newly acquired fame, however, still left Mary lacking money. She decided that perhaps she could acquire needed funds by going on a lecture tour. Her talks ranged from dress reform to health issues. She spoke about illnesses that could come from using tobacco or alcohol. She espoused the benefits of herbal medicines and homeopathic medicine. Every day, and for the rest of her life, Mary wore her medal whether she was speaking or not.

Due to her celebrity, Walker easily won election as president of the National Dress Reform Association. During her first talk to them she showed her humor by stating she knew of a fitting punishment for ex-Confederate President Jefferson Davis. "Treat him like a woman! He should be forced to wear hoop skirts and a tight corset, and do housework in a four-story home. This would be a worse punishment than any prison term."[14]

In the summer of 1866, Mary was chosen as delegate to the Woman's Social Science Convention in England. There she moved into a new controversy, as she gave a speech about women's suffrage which happened to make newspaper headlines. Her fame now opened the door for other speaking engagements abroad. Some were very well received while others were disrupted with booing or hooting.

Ironically, one account of Mary Walker's experience in Paris, France, was provided by the writings of Stafford native, Moncure Daniel

This photograph shows Mary in a rare pose with her hair down and wearing a lace collar.

Conway. Conway, the famous Southern emancipationist, was in Paris in 1867 experiencing France's Exposition. He wrote in his autobiography that he and other Americans were to attend two events to celebrate July 4th festivities. However, due to the death of Maximilian in Mexico, (See Chapter 2, pg. 20) one party was cancelled. While attending the one at the Grand Hotel with three hundred Americans present, he felt as if he had made the wrong decision by attending any festivity at all:

> Most of us were feeling the dinner dull, when suddenly Dr. Mary Walker extemporized a sensation. Over her famous "American dress" (masculine) she wore a large sash of stars and stripes; in this costume she walked up to the head of the table before the company, and before the amazed Milliken [master of ceremonies] could interfere, uttered a tribute to "Our soldiers and sailors," dramatically kissed the flag she wore, and glided to her seat. Dr. Mary Walker did not wait for the dancing that followed, and when she left received an ovation from the French crowd in the courtyard on account of the glorious independence of her trousers, nowise concealed but decorated by her patriotic sash. The applause must have been for Dr. Mary Walker's independence; uglier dress was never worn.[15]

After returning to America, Mary helped Susan B. Anthony and Lucy Stone organize the Women's Suffrage Association for Ohio. Later in 1868, she and well known suffragist, Belva Lockwood, supported a bill which would allow women in D.C. to vote. The bill failed.

Mary toured the country giving numerous speeches.

Despite the failure, Mary continued lecturing. She was paid for her speaking engagements, but her expenses, especially travel expenses, were so high that she found herself barely able to make ends meet. She asked her congressman to obtain a disability pension for her, since she felt her eyes were damaged while at Castle Thunder. Her request was denied, so she decided to print a book, entitled *Hit*, which was published in 1871. It reflected various views she normally expressed on her lecture tours, but this time she included her opinions on marriage and divorce.

Walker obtained some money from her book but still needed more funds. Being no less persistent than she had been during the war, Mary petitioned Congress at least twenty-five times for financial relief. She obtained a minor victory in 1874, for she was given a disability pension of $8.50 a month for her eye infirmity. Ironically, widows at that time, who had never served in the war, received at least that much or more.

In 1877, her father sold the family farm to Mary for $1,000.00. She found it difficult to raise the funds, yet she did. She did not live there, although her parents did. A year later she wrote another book, *The Science of Immorality*, which was written for men about marriage and infidelity.

Walker continued to give lecture tours, even though the end of the Civil War was a decade and a half earlier, and her audiences were dwindling. Therefore, Mary emphasized her views on women's suffrage. In 1881, Mary ran unsuccessfully for the U.S. Senate, an amazing feat considering women could not vote. A year later she obtained a job as a clerk in the mailroom of the Pensions Office. She did a very poor job and was out of the office due to sick leave about thirty-three percent of the time. After less than a year, she was dismissed from her position. Her life began a downward spiral.

Mary became a stage attraction for several years.

Needing funds, Mary stooped to working for vaudeville-type entertainment groups in 1887. She would give talks on such things as "Uses and Injuries of Tobacco" and receive $150 a week. Other featured groups on stage might be trained parrots, puppets, or fortune tellers. In March of 1893, the *Toledo Blade* criticized Mary by writing that she used to be on "the same platform with Presidents and the world's greatest women. There is something grotesque in her appearance [now] on a stage built for freaks."[16] Mary's sideshow act lasted several years.

Mary again asked the government for money she thought she justly deserved. Funds requested throughout Mary's many years of supplication were anywhere from ten thousand a month to fifty dollars a month. In 1898, when she was sixty-six years of age, she finally received twenty dollars a month.

Still having financial difficulty, Mary returned to Oswego to her family farm. Her father had since passed away, and she cared for her mother until her brother took over her care at his home. Mary tried to farm and sell produce, but this too was unsuccessful. Some concerned town citizens wrote the town board:

> Gentlemen, we hereby petition your honorable body to set apart the sum of five hundred dollars for the assistance of Dr. Mary E. Walker as an indigent nurse of the Civil War living within our town limits whom the law compels the town to support.[17]

To her horror, Mary's Medal of Honor was revoked in 1917.

In 1917, the worst thing that could ever happen to Mary took place when Congress revoked her Medal of Honor. Congress and the military revised the standards for the medal so that recipients had to have demonstrated extraordinary valor in "actual combat with an enemy." Along with Mary, 910 former recipients also had their medals revoked. Mary refused to give back her medals stating that she was, in fact, behind enemy lines when she helped nurse Confederate citizens. (In fact, Mary had two medals. One she originally received in 1865, and another she received in 1907, when the army issued medals with a new design.) Outraged, combative, eighty-five year old Mary went to the U.S. Capitol presumably to state her case. While there, she fell on the Capitol steps and never fully recovered.

Mary returned to Oswego a weakened woman. For a while she went to the United States General Hospital at Fort Ontario where her health appeared to improve. However, upon returning home she was still unable to care for herself. Therefore she spent her final days with a neighbor who recalled Mary saying, "Presidents and cabinet ministers and great generals were glad to meet and listen to me . . . But now I am alone with the infirmities of age fast weighing me down and practically penniless, and no one wants to bother with me."[18]

Mary Walker died two years after her fall, in 1919, at the age of eighty-seven. She was buried in a black suit at the family plot in Rural

Mary lacked financial assets in her later years.

Cemetery in Oswego. Ironically, a year after her death the Nineteenth Amendment to the Constitution was passed giving women the right to vote. In World War II a Liberty ship, the *SS Mary Walker*, was launched.

Mary would probably be very pleased if she were alive today, for women are actually voting and wearing pants. Scientists have discovered the dangers of both alcohol and tobacco and are encouraging people to use homeopathic medicine which she espoused. In June of 1977, after Mary's great grand-niece pleaded for her aunt's Medal of Honor to be restored, The Secretary of the Navy, under direction of President Jimmy Carter, reinstated Mary's Medal of Honor. It is currently on display in the Pentagon's women's corridor. At the present time, Mary is the only woman in the United States to have ever received the Medal of Honor. There are many places named in honor of Mary Walker such as the U.S. Army Reserve Center in Walker, Michigan; The Medical Facilities in Oswego, New York; and

the Mary E. Walker House in Coatsville, Pennsylvania, which serves veterans-in-need. In 1982, a United States stamp was issued in Oswego which commemorated her and her accomplishments. In 2000, the little doctor in pants was inducted into the Women's Hall of Fame in Seneca Falls, New York.

Mary Walker was honored with her image
on a United States postage stamp.

General Oliver Otis Howard

Founder of Howard University

*O*liver Otis Howard, despite suffering some humiliating defeats in the Civil War, is best remembered as "the Christian General." Surprisingly, his primary legacy lives today in educational institutions. He was the founder of Howard University, an African-American institution in Washington, D.C., and Lincoln Memorial University in Tennessee, for the education of "mountain whites."

Born November 8, 1830, in Leeds, Maine, Howard was raised in a "plain, two-story frame house" which was known around town as the residence of Captain Seth Howard, his grandfather. For a while Otis, as he was called by his father, lived on a small farm with his parents and grandfather. His grandfather, who was quite aged, helped Otis' mother around the house rather than his father in the field. Howard remembered, however, that his father, despite having little help, always supplied his family with food year round.

Howard grew up on the farm listening to his grandfather's military stories of the Revolutionary War. Otis also heard stories of his great-great grandfather, an aide to Miles Standish. In his autobiography, Howard later wrote with pride that it was a ". . . source of gratification to a man to find his family tree representing men exceptionally industrious and respectable."[1]

Otis was taught to read at an early age by his mother. At age four, he started going to a district school one mile south of his home. When five, his brother Rowland Bailey was born. About a year later, an event took place which changed his life forever. While on a trip to visit relatives in the Hudson Valley, his father returned home with a "little negro lad" whom he had befriended. This boy, Edward Johnson, lived with the family for four years. Both boys played and worked together on the farm. With fondness, Howard remembered them playing ball, shooting marbles, coasting, skating, and kiting together. Later he wrote, "I have always believed it a providential circumstance that I had that early experience with a negro lad, for it relieved me from that feeling of prejudice which would have hindered me from doing the work for the freedmen which, years afterwards, was committed to my charge."[2]

When Howard was eight years old, another brother, Charles, was born. Just a year later, his father died. This left his mother to care for three boys and the farm. Otis' grandfather moved in with another son, so his mother hired a "good strong Englishman" as a farm laborer.

One letter written by his mother always remained in Howard's memory throughout his life:

> I think if we cannot fill so high a station in life as we could desire, we may possibly do as much good in some less exacting situation. Our children, though humbly educated, may fill important stations in life. Let us hope for the best and bear with patience whatever crosses our path in life.[3]

Several years after his father's passing, Otis' mother remarried a "prosperous farmer" who had thee sons and lived six miles away. The Howard family joined Colonel John Gilmore's family and thus "began a new era."

At around eleven years of age, Otis was sent away to "high school." There he learned how to live away from home "without too much homesickness." Later his mother's brother, Hon. John Otis, offered him a place to live if he would do chores, such as taking care of his horse and cow. Howard lived with his aunt and uncle and was taken in by them as a son. This enabled Otis to attend Mr. Burnham's advanced high school of six young men who learned Latin and Greek. During off times, Otis would go back to his step-father's farm and work. The young student was later accepted at Monmouth Academy in preparation for college. He would board away from home again. While departing for school, his mother said, "Do the best you can, Otis, with your studies, and try hard to do right, ever seeking God's help."[4] He said that his mother often repeated this message in her letters throughout his student life.

Otis attended Bowdoin College at the age of fifteen.

Otis' studies at college-preparatory schools were successful and at the young age of fifteen he took tests and was accepted at Bowdoin College in Brunswick, Maine. (Distinguished alumni included President Franklin Pierce and American authors Longfellow and Hawthorne.) Periodically, he would stay out of college and teach school to aid his mother with tuition. While at Bowdoin, he met a roommate's cousin, Elizabeth Ann Waite, otherwise known as Lizzie. They fell in love but decided to wait for marriage until Otis could complete four years at West Point.

At first the Army academy was a rough on Otis, and he wrote about the "fatiguing drills with [a] fifteen pound musket."[5] Also, his social life was trying, as some fellow cadets shunned him for his religious nature. Eventually, he worked out his difficulties and toward the end of his time at the academy he wrote his mother that he loved West Point "almost as much as I used to hate it." While at West Point he was active in a Bible study class and the Dialectic Society, a cadet literary and debating society. Once Howard fell in the gymnasium and ended up in the hospital. The superintendent of the academy, Colonel Robert E. Lee, visited him and sat down by his bedside and spoke to him "very kindly." Later, when out of the hospital, Howard and his dear friend and fellow cadet, Jeb Stuart, visited Colonel Lee's family and were "well received by every member of it."[6] Howard successfully graduated from West Point, fourth in a class of forty-six, unaware that less than ten years later, many of his academy friends would be on opposite sides of a devastating civil war.

At graduation, Otis received a commission as a brevet second lieutenant. (This was the practice allowing graduates to serve while awaiting official vacancies.) Since he ranked so high in his class he could choose which branch of the army he wished to serve. He chose the Ordnance Department, primarily because all the arsenals, magazines, and armories throughout the county had quarters for married officers. He reported for duty at Watervliet Arsenal in West Troy, New York on September, 1854. Less than a half a year later, in February of 1854, Howard was given twenty days leave for his marriage to Lizzie in Maine. After their honeymoon, the newlyweds settled into Watervliet. Just a few months later, they were transferred Kennebee Arsenal at Augusta, Maine. Reluctant to leave their first home in New York, they happily discovered that the new quarters in Maine were beautiful. December of that year their first child, Guy, was born. While in Augusta, Howard spent his leisure time training horses.

The family soon returned to Watervliet. This time their household increased, as they were joined by Otis' mother, his mother-in-law, and his brother, Rowland Bailey, R.B. R.B. would use their house as a base while attending law school in Albany. Howard wrote, "Everything went on smoothly until the latter part of December, 1856." He was shocked as "I would have been by a clap of thunder from a clear sky, by an order from Washington."[7] He was ordered to report immediately to Tampa, Florida, and could not bring his family.

In Tampa, Howard had a small office building near the arsenal which he set up as his sleeping room. Colonel L.L. Loomis, 5th Infantry, became the commander of the department. Loomis was a member of the Presbyterian Church and gave Otis books, booklets, and tracts to read. He once told him, "Howard, you have an inquiring mind." While "absorbing" the reading material, he heard from R.B. that he had given up his law studies and gone into the ministry. On the night of May 31, 1857, Howard had a remarkable religious experience. He wrote that reading the scripture from the first epistle of John, "The blood of Christ cleanseth us from all sin," had changed his life. He now felt "he was a different man, with different hopes and different purposes in life."[8] Later, he poignantly wrote:

> The joy of that night was so great that it would be difficult to attempt in any way to describe it. The next morning everything appeared to me to be changed – the sky was brighter, the trees more beautiful, and the songs of the birds were never before so sweet to my ears.[9]

While in Florida, Howard heard the Army was to "close out the war with the Seminoles," but there had been no great battle. However, he did witness many deaths on base due to "sickness" that summer. While there, he was very happy to receive a letter that his second child, Grace Ellen, was born. Eight months later, Otis received orders to return to New York where he would be an instructor of mathematics at West Point.

Howard returned to West Point to teach mathematics to the cadets.

His family moved into a small cottage on post, and Otis settled into his teaching duties. He also formed a group of cadets into a "social meeting for prayer and conference" that was held twice a week after supper. Starting out with five, the group grew until nearly half the corps of cadets became members. Later, a Young Men's Christian Association, (YMCA) chapter was formed and took charge of the meetings.

Otis stayed at West Point from 1857 – 1861, becoming a first lieutenant in 1858. In 1861, there was quite a disturbance on campus as "cotton state cadets and officers" were leaving to head south. Howard defined his view of the ethic of the "old army."

> We belong to the whole nation, we do not want it divided; we propose to stand
> by it forever, but we do hate this civil strife; we will not be eager to enter the lists
> in such a conflict; certainly not merely for the sake of promotion. We do hope
> and pray that the differences will be settled without bloodshed.[10]

After much prayer, Howard decided to leave West Point and resign his regular army commission to accept a position as a colonel commanding the 3rd Regiment of Maine Volunteers. Such moves involved risk for Regular Army officers who, in effect, lost their established positions in the Army. He wrote, "I gave up every other plan except as to the best way for me to contribute to the saving of her [the nation's] life."[11]

Leaving his family at West Point, Howard traveled by train to Augusta, Maine, to pick up his men. While at the Augusta House Hotel, he was surprised to see his brother, the theological student. Charles had quit seminary and offered "himself for enlistment." Shortly thereafter, he became a second lieutenant in the 61st New York Infantry. He later became his brother's aide-de-camp and remained by his side until 1865. His other brother, R.B. was a Congregational minister, so Otis was hoping the regiment would elect him as chaplain but instead voted for another. So R.B. "went to the front as an agent of the Christian Commission."

Otis met his regiment, initially 1,000 strong, across the street from the statehouse encamped in a park. He attempted some essential drilling to enable him to move the regiment in-body to Washington, D.C., with "some degree of precision." Not given much time, the newly formed group had to move on June 5, 1861. Howard described the day as beautiful with not a cloud in the sky and "luxurious lilacs were in full bloom." He noted that the "dresses of women and children furnished every variety of coloring, and little by little the people grouped themselves along the slope of the Kennebee River."[12] Men with "bright-buttoned uniforms" started saying goodbye to their loved ones. After the regimental band "struck up a national air," the train, packed with men, slowly moved out from Augusta.

Along the way, the train received "abundant cheering and words of encourage-ment" at the various railroad stations. When they pulled into the large depot at Brunswick, where Bowdoin College was located, Howard was surprised see professors, as well as students, in the crowd. At Portland, Maine's largest city, people went into the train cars and "freely offered" food, drink, and flowers to the soldiers of the 3rd.

By the time the regiment reached Boston, they unloaded from the cars and went to Boston Common where they were welcomed. They had the "choicest supper" which was spread out on many tables. Howard wrote, "My thousand men were never better fed or served, because mothers and daughters of Massachusetts were ministering to them."[13] In Boston they boarded a large steamer and traveled to New York. Once there, in a large drill hall of the armory, Howard's troops removed their knapsacks and arranged them as seats. The "Sons of Maine" presented the men with a regimental flag and a delicious dinner. Philadelphia also was welcoming with good food and "patriotic spirit." However, the welcoming at Baltimore, Maryland was quite different. (Although Maryland had been coerced to remain in the Union, Baltimore openly supported the South.) A few days before their arrival, the 6th Massachusetts had incurred bloody riots in the streets, so Howard's men were escorted off the trains by police escorts. Marching in columns they went from station to station, a distance of about two miles. They boarded a steamer, and on the evening of June 7th, they pulled into Washington, D.C.

Howard wanted to contribute by "saving the nation's life."

The regiment was met at the dock and taken to a vacant building on Pennsylvania Avenue. Awaiting the men was "a bare floor, a chair-less room without table or lights," and "a cold reception, a depressing welcome to their beloved capital, for whose preservation they had been ready to fight to the death."[14] The next morning, feeling so sorry for the homesick boys, Howard arranged to give the entire regiment a breakfast at Willard's Hotel for fifty cents a man. He admitted later that he "lacked wisdom and ordinary reasoning," since he thus became personally responsible for the large amount. But, at the time, he felt a greater urgency to satisfy "the need of removing at any cost a universal depression."[15]

After the extravagant breakfast, the regiment marched along Pennsylvania Avenue and Fourteenth Street to Meridian Hill. The heat was intense and the men were loaded down with their knapsacks, haversacks, and cartridge boxes. Some stopped by the wayside to rest or get water. Halfway along the march, which continued until dark, a storm arose accompanied by "wind, fierce lightning, and pouring rain." Howard later wrote, "Thus that short five-mile march was the beginning of the hardships and experiences of real war."[16]

Fortunately, other regiments who were already on Meridian Hill were willing to house Howard's wet men for the night. The next day tents were pitched and the regiment settled in. About three weeks later, suddenly without any warning symptoms, Howard suffered from an attack of "something like cholera." With the doctor's care, his brother Charles' love, and "the blessing of God" Otis got better. Later, he learned that President Lincoln had called twice at his tent when he was unconscious.

The first part of July, Howard heard that the War Department was directing him to select three regiments in addition to his own and form a brigade; but, first he was to take his regiment to Alexandria, Virginia. Traveling by steamer his men unloaded only to find "Alexandria was more gloomy than Baltimore." Most residences, beautiful homes, and stores were deserted. Grass, foliage, and flowers had been trampled by previous troop movements. Howard went back to Washington while his men settled in and selected the 4th Maine, 5th Maine, and the 2nd Vermont Regiments to form his new brigade.

The brigade moved to Manassas and participated in the First Battle of Bull Run. Afterwards, in September, Howard was promoted to brigadier general. His brigade subsequently joined Major General George McClellan's Army of the Potomac and participated in the Peninsula Campaign. While outside of Richmond, Howard's brigade participated in the Battle of Fair Oaks Station or as the Confederates called it, the Battle at Seven Pines. On June 1, 1862, the second day of battle, Howard was wounded "through the right forearm by a small Mississippi rifle ball." His brother ran to him saying that his horse had been shot from under him. Charles immediately took a handkerchief and bound up his brother's arm and returned to battle. Otis, regardless of his wound, pressed forward too. Not long afterwards, he was shot again in the same right arm, but this time his elbow was shattered. With bullets flying overhead, he was placed on the ground where a medical director bound up his arm. Charles found his brother, but he was limping and using his empty scabbard for a cane, for he had been shot through the thigh. The doctor dressed Charles' leg and put him on a stretcher, but Otis decided to walk. They found shelter at a nearby home where a "negro cabin" was used as an operating room. When told by the brigade surgeon that his arm would have to be amputated above the elbow, Howard said, "All right, go ahead. [I'm] happy to lose only my arm."[17]

The next morning, both brothers were driven to the Fair Oaks Station with the surgeon's certificate of disability in hand. There they ran into General Philip Kearny. Kearny and Howard grasped hands. Kearny had lost his left arm in Mexico. To console Howard he said, "General, I am sorry for you; but you must not mind it; the ladies will not think the less of you." Glancing at his missing hand, Otis replied, "There is one thing that we can do, general, we can buy our gloves together!"[18] Laughing, the two departed.

Howard lost his arm at the Battle of Fair Oaks/Seven Pines.

Jostling in a freight-car bed covered with straw, the wounded brothers endured a long three-hour trip to White House Landing, where they boarded a steamer which would take them up the York River and then on to Baltimore. At a Baltimore wharf they were driven three agonizing miles over cobblestones to the railroad station. After more than a year's separation, the reunion in an Auburn hotel with Howard's wife and children was wonderful. Just ten days after the reunion, however, he was giving speeches throughout Maine. After a two months and twenty days absence, Howard returned to the field in time to participate in the closing operations of the Second Bull Run campaign. During the Battle of Antietam, in September of 1862, Howard's brigade was ambushed in the West Woods. Later during the battle, after General Sedgwick was wounded, Otis took control of Sedgwick's Division, II Army Corps.

That November, Howard was in Warrenton with General Burnside, the new commander of the Army of the Potomac. Burnside discovered that Lee and half of his Confederate Army were now in Gordonsville and Culpeper. Burnside planned to advance toward Lee and then shift rapidly to capture Fredericksburg using pontoon bridges. Therefore, he asked General-in-Chief, Major General Halleck to order pontoon bridging to be moved from Berlin, Maryland, and D.C. south to the Rappahannock for his planned attack.

Burnside's army, including Howard's division, left Warrenton on November 15, 1862. The first day they marched to Hartwood and encamped at Spotted Tavern. The next day they made an easy trek into Falmouth town. On their way to Stafford Heights they were spotted by a few Confederates in Fredericksburg. Shots rang out only to be silenced as the Rebels noticed the long stream of Yankees and abandoned their plans.

When Burnside arrived he was very upset that the pontoon boats and bridges were not in Stafford. Both Generals Hooker and Sumner thought that since there were few troops in Fredericksburg, they could easily cross the river and seize the town. But, Burnside thought that the rising river caused too great a threat and decided to wait for the bridges. While in Stafford, on November 29th, Howard was promoted to major general.

Delays in pontoon bridges arriving at Falmouth allowed Lee to move his army, Longstreet's corps from Gordonsville and Jackson's corps from Winchester, to Fredericksburg. Taking advantage of the situation, Lee placed his troops "in a semicircle along the Fredericksburg Heights." They were preparing a deadly reception for the Union soldiers.

While in Stafford, Howard was promoted to Major General.

Finally, by December 11th, the waiting was over and the pontoon boats, planking, and equipment had arrived. After building bridges lower on the Rappahannock, the Federal engineers attempted to build a bridge directly below the Lacy House (Chatham). Confederate sharpshooters thwarted their efforts despite heavy artillery firing from Stafford Heights. Finally, Hall's brigade of Howard's division used the pontoons as boats and assaulted the town and rooted out the sharpshooters. This enabled the bridge to be completed. Howard described what happened next:

My corps commander (Couch) next ordered me to take my entire division over and clear that part of the town near our advance of all Confederates, and so secure a safe transit for the remainder of our corps.[19]

Howard found Fredericksburg much damaged by the Union shelling but was shocked to discover that many citizens were still in town who had spent the day sheltered in cellars.

In the evening while making inspections, he ran across some Union soldiers who were playing musical instruments, singing, and dancing. He thought this was unusual preparation for battle the next day. They replied, "Ah, general, let us sing and dance to-night; we will fight the better for it to-morrow!"[20] However, on December 12th Howard wrote, "There was no actual battle; but there was considerable artillery practice and some brisk skirmishing."[21]

The morning of the 13th found Howard, his brother Charles, and other officers in the abandoned Knox house. Scripture was read and prayers said when a little old lady made her way to the general. She seemed moved that Howard said prayerfully that they would conquer. The woman, referring to three Confederate generals replied, "You will have a Stone wall to encounter, Hills to climb, and a Long street to tread before you can succeed."[22] (This story has been included in numerous other "first person" accounts. It is not clear whether it originally happened to Howard.) The old woman certainly foretold the future, as Union troops experienced massive losses with 12,653 casualties compared with the Confederate casualties of 4,576.

After the terrible defeat, the Union crossed the Rappahannock and limped back to Stafford. Howard and his tired, sad, and dejected men returned to the same encampments they had left several days before. Throughout January, Howard noted that there were many desertions. On January 20-24 they had participated in the abortive "Mud March" resulting in a humiliating failure. Burnside was dismissed, and on January 26th, Lincoln placed "Fighting Joe" Hooker in command of the Army of the Potomac. He reorganized and revitalized the army emphasizing better care of the troops, giving them fresh bread, vegetables, meat, and new uniforms. He had them drill and do target practice. Howard noted, "Hooker . . . by his prompt and energetic measures, soon changed the whole tone of the army for the better."[23]

One of the other changes Hooker made was to rearrange the army into eight corps. Upon hearing that General Hooker placed General Sickles in charge of the Third Corps, Howard immediately wrote a letter to Hooker. Thinking he had been overlooked as Sickles was his junior, Howard asked that he be given an assignment according to his rank. At the end of March, General Sigel was replaced, and Howard assumed command of the XI Army Corps which was stationed around Stafford Courthouse. Here he found a force that was about "13,000 strong. It had about 5,000 Germans and 8,000 Americans." He met a cordial reception, but not a warm one, as many of the German men missed a commander, like Sigel, who spoke German.

Captain Charles Howard was an aide to his brother. This picture was taken in Falmouth.

In April, Lincoln visited the army in Stafford and received many reviews. On the 10th, Howard's XI Corps was reviewed by the president. Following the review, Lincoln went to the courthouse where he had "very good entertainment, cold meats, etc." Howard later recalled the president's visit to his tent:

> The German troops had made a long bower in front of it, and he could not get in without taking off his hat – he was so tall. He came in and sat on my bedstead. I had a fur robe. It was the skin of a South American sheep. He admired it as it lay on my bed. I had a set of tablets for the week hanging at the end of my tent. They were supposed to be changed every day. The one that was hanging there at the time was part of the 23rd Psalm – "The Lord is My Shepherd. I shall not want." He talked about it.[24]

The XI Corps stayed in the courthouse area awaiting orders. Howard wrote that, "General Hooker had managed to keep his plans in his own bosom." But on April 25th, Howard was alerted for movement and ordered that his men "had on hand eight days' rations in knapsacks and haversacks." Hooker ended the instructions by writing, "I am directed to inform you confidentially, for your own information and not for publication, that your whole corps will probably move . . . as early as Monday a.m."[25]

Gradually, one corps at a time left Stafford and traveled west on Warrenton Road to various fords in order to cross into enemy territory. Howard's corps was one of the first to head to Kelly's Ford. Soldiers found travel extremely difficult as each was intentionally loaded with fifty-six to sixty pounds of food, minimal clothing, and ammunition.[26]

Howard's corps, along with two other corps, crossed the Rappahannock at Kelly's Ford. Moving with the XII Corps, they crossed the Rapidan at Germanna Ford and finally arrived in the Chancellorsville area. General Hooker ordered Howard's corps to defend the right flank of the Union army. Howard described this Wilderness area, "Except the small openings, the forest was continuous and nearly enveloping. Generally the trees were near together with entanglements of undergrowth."[27]

Hooker reduced the XI Corps by ordering some of Howard's men to defend other areas. At six o'clock in the evening, on May 2nd, Howard described "Stonewall" Jackson's surprise attack:

> I heard the first murmuring of a coming storm – a little quick firing on the picket line, the wild rushing of frightened game into our very camps, and almost sooner than it can be told the bursting of thousands of Confederates through the almost impenetrable thickets of the wilderness and then the wilder, nosier conflict which ensured. It was a terrible gale . . . the dead and dying in sight and the wounded straggling along; the frantic efforts of the brave and patriotic to stay the angry storm.[28]

Lee had "out-flanked" the Federal effort to "out-flank" him and had won his greatest victory. After Chancellorsville, Howard wrote, "It has been customary to blame me and my corps for the disaster."[29] However, he felt that he followed orders and was left with too few men. He recalled:

> . . . on that terrible day of May 2, 1863, I did all which could have been done by a corps commander in the presence of that panic of men largely caused by the overwhelming attack of Jackson's 26,000 men against my isolated corps of 8,000 without its reserve – thus outnumbering me 3 to 1.[30]

Howard's corps returned to Stafford, this time encamped near Brooke Station. After leaving Stafford in mid-June, 1863, the XI Corps next fought in Gettysburg in July. This is where Howard suffered his second great military setback. His corps lost 3,000 men in which half of them were captured while the enemy had only suffered 1,000 casualties. Howard was given thanks by Congress, however, for he recommended that the I and XI Corps go to a strategic location on Culp's Hill and Cemetery Ridge thus helping the Union win the battle.

In the fall of 1863, Howard's XI Corps and the XII Corps were sent west to Chattanooga under Hooker. May through September of 1864 found Howard commanding the IV Corps in the Atlanta Campaign. Afterwards, General Sherman made him commander of the Army of the Tennessee. Howard finished the war fighting with those men during Sherman's Carolinas' Campaign from January through April of 1865.

Howard rode in the Grand Review in Washington, D.C.

In May of 1865, the victorious Union Army planned to have a two day Grand Review in Washington, D.C. Several days before the review, Sherman met privately with Howard asking him to relinquish riding in the review with his men. Instead he wanted General Logan to take the lead. Howard was very hurt by this request and said, "I had maneuvered and fought this army from Atlanta, all the way through." To this Sherman replied, "Howard, you are a Christian, and won't mind such a sacrifice." Howard said, "Surely, if you put it on that ground, I submit." On May 24th, Howard was going to ride with his staff, but Sherman called him up to ride with him.[31] He later wrote of the incident:

> I rode with him amid the cheers of the people, until approaching the reviewing stand, then I rode over to his right, so that he might face the president [Lincoln] while he saluted. I did not draw my sword, but I had a habit of riding with my reins in my teeth, and raised my hat and saluted and drove by.[32]

After the review, the Howard family, now comprised of Otis, Lizzie, and four children, settled in a home located in downtown Washington, D.C. Howard was appointed a brigadier general in the Regular Army, thus returning to the career service.

Two months before the Washington Grand Reviews, on March 3, 1865, President Lincoln had signed an act establishing the Bureau of Refugees, Freedmen and Abandoned Lands. Afterwards, on a May evening, Howard was requested to meet with Secretary of War Edwin Stanton at the War Department. Sitting in the secretary's office Howard was handed a copy of the act and Stanton told him:

> Mr. Lincoln before his death expressed a decided wish that you should have the office [Commissioner of the Bureau]; but he was not willing to detail you till you could be spared from the army in the field. Now, as the war is ended, the way is clear. The place will be given you if you are willing to attempt it.[33]

Howard humbly accepted the position. In his writings Howard explained who these "freedmen" and "refugees" were:

> It was not the negroes alone who were so thoroughly shaken up and driven hither and thither by the storms of war. Those named in the South the "poor whites," especially of the mountain regions of Georgia, Tennessee, North and South Carolina, were included. These had all along been greatly divided in their allegiance – some for the union, and some for the Confederacy . . . To these two classes, negroes and whites, were usually given the names of freedmen and refugees.[34]

Howard served as "Freedmen's Bureau" commissioner for nine years. He tried to house, educate, clothe, and give medical assistance to these individuals. He also attempted to distribute abandoned lands in many states. Unfortunately, over the years, the Bureau drifted from Lincoln's grand vision and Howard's control, as it became corrupt and inefficient. In 1874, Howard went before a board of inquiry. Legal expenses alone cost him $7,000. Howard was eventually exonerated and completely vindicated. However, Howard biographer John A. Carpenter, wrote that, "The cost was great also in damaged reputation, to himself and to the cause for which he had worked."[35]

While heading the bureau, on November 20, 1866, Howard had met with ten individuals representing various charitable groups to discuss the formation of a seminary which would train "negro" ministers. Broadening the concept, it was decided instead to form the Howard Normal and Theological Institute for the Education of Preachers and Teachers. On January 8th of the next year, the Board of Trustees voted to change the name of the institute to Howard University and shortly thereafter it was incorporated by Congress. Howard concurrently held the office as president from 1867 until 1874.

This two and a half story home was built by Howard for his large family.
It is on the present site of Howard University.

In 1868, the Howard family, which now included a two year old son, had moved into a large house overlooking Washington, D.C. The following year a sixth child was born. In 1871, their last child was born making a sixteen year age difference between their eldest and youngest child.

Settling in the capital city, Howard helped organize and raise money for the First Congregational Church. However, in 1869, Howard endured more conflict and controversy when he tried to introduce blacks into the church.

In 1874, General Howard was placed in command of the Department of the Columbia. This took in all of Washington, Oregon, a part of Idaho, and included within its limits the Territory of Alaska. He traveled to Fort Vancouver six miles from Portland and west of the Columbia River. It was here, in the northwest, where he fought in the Indian Wars. One of the most famous, in 1877 against the Nez Perces, was summarized by Howard in his autobiography:

> In the Nez Perces campaign I gathered all available military forces near Fort Lapwal, Idaho, and after the most arduous campaign, with several battles and a continuous march of over 1,400 miles across the Rocky Mountains, making our way through the forests of the Yellowstone National Park, I succeeded in detaining the Indians till General Nelson A. Miles overtook and had a battle with them near Bearjaw Mountain. The firing was still going on when I arrived on the field, and through my own interpreters succeeded in persuading Chief Joseph to abandon further hostile effort and make a prompt surrender.[36]

Chief Joseph was urged to surrender through Howard's interpreters.

Howard and his family lived near Portland, Oregon, until 1881. While there he attended church in Portland and participated in many Y.M.C.A. activities. He felt very strongly about the organization, for he had worked with them while in Washington, D.C., and they had originated the U.S. Christian Commission of Civil War-fame. It was at one of their meetings in Oregon that he gave his first talk about his Gettysburg experiences. Later in life, he would travel around the nation giving speeches about his Civil War activities.

In 1881-82 Howard became Superintendent of West Point. After his time there, the family moved to Omaha, Nebraska. In 1884, he obtained leave of absence and traveled to Germany where he met his third child, Jamie, who was studying in Antwerp, Belgium. Together they toured Europe, Greece, Egypt and Constantinople. In 1886, while still in Omaha, Otis was promoted to Major General and given orders to go to San Francisco, California and "assume command of the military division which then embraced the entire Pacific coast."[37] Later, the family moved to New York where Howard commanded the Division of the East at Governor's Island. While in New York, he would visit "my old and beloved commander," General Sherman who lived in that city.

In 1893, Howard received the Medal of Honor for bravery at Fair Oaks/Seven Pines, the place where he lost his arm 31 years' earlier. A year later, he retired and the family settled in Burlington, Vermont.

Consistent with his earlier Freedmen's Bureau work and founding Howard University, Howard established the Lincoln Memorial University at Harrogate, Tennessee in 1895. The school offered a college education to the mountain people of the area. Later in his life Howard wrote, "The organizing of the institution, the raising of the funds for its plant, the establishment of an endowment, and keeping up the running expenses have been . . . a decided labor of love."[38] It also was a fitting tribute to Abraham Lincoln, whom Howard had revered.

This photograph was taken about a year before Howard's death.

President Theodore Roosevelt, in 1905, asked Howard to participate in his inauguration. Otis commanded the veterans and rode in a special review in front of the Capitol.

Oliver Otis Howard died on October 26, 1909 in Burlington, just two weeks before his 79th birthday. He died quickly as he had wished, for he told his son Harry, "Some day it [heart] will just stop and I will be on the other shore."[39] He was buried with full military honors in Lake View Cemetery. Howard had written what arguably would remain as his most enduring eulogy. At the end of his autobiography he wrote, "It is a fitting close to my life story to lift up my heart in thanksgiving to my Heavenly Father for the mercies and blessings which he has unceasingly showered upon me and mine."[40]

Howard's many accomplishments are best remembered in the two schools he founded, the bust by James E. Kelly on display at Howard University, and by the statue of him on horseback at the Gettysburg Battlefield. A dormitory at his beloved Bowdoin College is named for him as well as an Army Reserve Center in Auburn, Maine.

Howard's equestrian statue can be found on East Cemetery Hill on the Gettysburg Battlefield.

NOTES

GENERAL DANIEL SIKLES; Colorful and Controversial

1   W.A. Swanberg, *Sickles the Incredible.* (New York: Charles Scribner's Sons, 1956) 5.

2   Virginia Clay-Clopton, *A Belle of the Fifties: The Memoirs of Mrs. Clay of Alabama.* (New York: Doubleday, Page & Co., 1905) 97-98.

3   Nat Brandt, *The Congressman Who Got Away with Murder* (New York: Syracuse University Press, 1991) 122-23.

4   Swanberg 55.

5   Swanberg 59.

6   F. Stansbury Haydon, *Military Ballooning during the Early Civil War.* (Baltimore: The Johns Hopkins University Press, 1941) 278.

7   *The Fredericksburg Herald*, April 4, 1862.

8   *Richmond Daily Enquirer*, April 9, 1862.

9   Jane Hollenbeck Conner, *Lincoln in Stafford.* (Fredericksburg: Cardinal Press, 2006) 50-51.

10   Princess Felix Salm-Salm, *Ten Years of my Life* (New York: R. Worthington, 1877) 41.

11   William B. Styple, *Generals in Bronze; Revealing Interviews with the Commanders of the Civil War.* (Kearny, NJ: Belle Grove Publishing Co., 2005) 98.

12   Styple, 98.

13   Styple 177-78.

14   David Ford, "Daniel Edgar Sickles" *On Point, the Journal of Army History.* Summer 2007, Vol 13, No 1, pg. 22.

15   Swanberg 378.

16   Swanberg 379.

17   Styple 162.

18   *The New York Times*, May 4, 1914

19   *The New York Times*, May 9, 1914.

PRINCESS AGNES SALM-SALM; Righteous, Regal, or Relentless?

1   Princess Felix Salm-Salm, *Ten Years of my Life.* (New York: R. Worthington, 1877) 20.

2   Salm-Salm 20-21.

3   Salm-Salm 21.

4   Salm-Salm 26.

5   Salm-Salm 32.

6   Salm-Salm 35.

7   Salm-Salm 38.

8   Salm-Salm 39.

9   Ibid.

10   Salm-Salm 40.

11   Carl Sandburg, *Abraham Lincoln*; The War Years. vol. 2 (NY: Harcourt, Brace & World, Inc. 1939) 84.

12   Salm-Salm 44.

13   Salm-Salm 67.

14   Salm-Salm 96.

15   David Coffey, *Soldier Princess*. (TX: Texas A & M University Press, 2002) 23.

16   Salm-Salm 103.

17   Salm-Salm 121

18   Salm-Salm 69.

19   Salm-Salm 72.

20   *The New York Times*, October 2, 1876.

21   Des Moines *Iowa State Register*, May 4, 1899. Coffey, 8.

22   *The New York Times*, May 15, 1899.

23   Coffey 91.

24   *The New York Times*, March 30, 1900.

25   William E. Barton, *The Life of Clara Barton*. vol. 2 (New York: AMS Press, 1969) 279. (A collection of their letters can be found in *The Clara Barton Collection* at the Library of Congress and another microfiche copy at the NPS Clara Barton home site in Glen Echo, MD)

26   Dumas Malone, Ed. *Dictionary of American Biography*, vol 8. (New York: Charles Scribner's Sons, 1963) 311.

27   Coffey 92.

CLARA BARTON; Angel of the Battlefield

1   William E. Barton, *The Life of Clara Barton; Founder of the American Red Cross*. Vol. 1 (New York: AMS Press, 1922) 6-7.

2   Barton 27.

3   Barton 21.

4   Barton 29-30.

5   Barton 35.

6   Barton 36.

7   Barton 37.

8   Barton 49.

9   Barton 57.

10   Barton 66.

11   Barton 95.

12   Barton 109.

13   Barton 123.

14   Barton 125-26.

15   Elizabeth Brown Pryor, *Clara Barton; Professional Angel*. (Philadelphia: University of Pennsylvania Press (1987) 1990) 84.

16   Elizabeth Brown Pryor, *Clara Barton; Official National Park Handbook.* (Washington, D.C: Division of Publications, National Park Service, 1981) 60.

17   Barton 159.

18   Barton 164-165.

19   Stephen B. Oates, *A Woman of Valor; Clara Barton and the Civil War* (New York: The Free Press, 1994) 53.

20   Oates 57.

21   Barton, 177.

22   Pryor, *Professional Angel* 89.

23   Barton 180.

24   Barton 195-96.

25   Barton 209.

26   Charles Wolcott, *History of the Twenty-First Regiment Massachusetts.* 213-214.

27   Barton 210.

28   Barton 210-11.

29   Barton 213.

30   Oates 102.

31   Barton 214.

32   Barton 215.

33   Barton 212-13.

34   Clara Barton Diaries & Correspondence, Microfilm Reel #63, Library of Congress, Civil war Manuscript Collection, Letter dated, March 29, 1863.

35   Barton 216.

36   Barton 217.

37   Barton 218.

38   Barton 218.

39   Pryor 106.

40   Pryor 107.

41   Clara Barton Diaries & Correspondence, Microfilm Reel #63, Library of Congress, Civil War Manuscript Collection, Letter dated December 3, 1863.

42   Barton 219.

43   Newspaper clipping, Fredericksburg and Spotsylvania. NPS, BV 465 and Oates 115.

44   Barton 219.

45   Oates 110.

46   Oates 117.

47   Oates 112.

48   Oates 118.

49   Oates 113.

50   Barton 222.

51   Barton 223.

52   Oates 124.

53 Clara Barton Diaries & Correspondence, Microfilm Reel #63, Library of Congress, Civil War Manuscript Collection. Letter dated January 18, 1863.

54 Barton 220.

55 Ibid.

56 Barton 230.

57 Barton 273.

58 Barton 274.

59 Ibid.

60 Barton 275.

61 Barton 276.

62 Barton 277.

63 Barton 277-78.

64 Barton 278-79.

65 Barton 279.

66 Clara Barton Diaries & Correspondence, Microfilm Reel #54, Library of Congress, Civil War Manuscript Collection. Letter written to Clara by Honora Connors, Feb. 15, 1897.

67 Clara Barton Diaries & Correspondence, Microfilm Reel #63, Library of Congress, Civil War Manuscript Collection. Diary entry, May 22, 1864.

68 Barton 279.

69 Barton 289.

70 Barton 300.

71 Barton 304.

72 Pryor 179.

73 Barton Introduction xi.

WALT WHITMAN; The Good Gray Poet.

1 David S. Reynolds. *Walt Whitman's America* (New York: Alfred A. Knopf, Inc., 1995), 24.

2 Reynolds 21.

3 Reynolds 58.

4 Reynolds 60.

5 Reynolds 68.

6 Reynolds 134.

7 Reynolds 311.

8 Reynolds 148.

9 Moncure Daniel Conway, Autobiography; Memories and Experiences, vol. 1 (Boston: Houghton, Mifflin and Co., 1904) 216.

10 Conway 215-16.

11 Conway 216.

12   Reynolds 152.

13   Reynolds 153.

14   Conway 216.

15   Conway 217.

16   Conway 218.

17   Charles I. Glicksberg, *Walt Whitman and the Civil War*
      (New York: A.S. Barnes and Co., 1963) 17.

18   Robert Roper, *Now the Drum of War* (New York: Walker & Company, 2008) 124

19   Candice Ward, Ed. *Walt Whitman: Civil War Poetry and Prose*
      (Mineola, NY: Dover Pub., 1995) 60.

20   Jerome M. Loving, Ed. *The Civil War Letters of George Washington Whitman*
      (Durham, NC: Duke State University Press, 1975) Letter, Dec. 16, 1862.

21   Glicksberg 69-70.

22   Ward 41.

23   Glicksburg 70.

24   Ward 62. Letter written to Nat Bloom and Fred Gray, March 19, 1863.

25   *New York Herald*, December 21, 1862.

26   Glicksberg 68-69.

27   Glicksberg 73.

28   Glicksberg 73-74.

29   Glicksberg 74.

30   Glicksberg 81.

31   Glicksberg 75.

32   Ward 19.

33   From "Return of a Brooklyn Veteran", Clicksberg 88.

34   Reynolds 455.

35   Reynolds 439.

36   Reynolds 474.

37   Conway, Whitman Letter inserted between 218 and 219.

38   Reynolds 528.

39   Reynolds 550.

40   Reynolds 586.

41   Reynolds 588.

42   Reynolds 588

43   Reynolds 588-89.

DR. MARY EDWARDS WALKER; A Woman Doctor in Pants

1   Robert Werlich, "Mary Walker: From Union Army Surgeon to Side Show Freak" *Civil War Times Ilustrated* (1967) 46.

2   Allen Mikaelian, *Medal of Honor: Profiles of America's Military Heroes from the Civil War to the Present* (New York: Hyperion, 2002) 5

3   Werlich 46.

4   Carla Joinson, "Mary Walker: A woman ahead of her time" *Free Lance-Star* (Fredericksburg: 2006) 7.

5   Elizabeth D. Leonard, *Yankee Women; Gender Battles in the Civil War* (New York: W.W. Norton & Co.1992) 116.

6   General Ambrose Burnside to "To Whom it May Concern," 15 November 1862, War Department Records

7   *The New York Tribune* article was quoted in the *Oswego Times*, May 9, 1863

8   Mercedes Graf, *A Woman of Honor: Dr. Mary E. Walker and the Civil War* (Gettysburg, PA: Thomas Publications, 2001) 36.

9   Graf 36-37.

10 Moncure Daniel Conway, *Autobiography; Memories and Experiences of Moncure Daniel Conway in Two Volumes.*" vol. 2, (Boston: Houghton, Mifflin and Company, 1904.) 175.

11 Mikaelian 8.

12 Mikaelian 10.

13 Mary's letter to her mother - published in *New York Times* June 16, 1864

14 Joinson 87.

15 Conway, vol. 2, 175.

16 Werlich 49.

17 Joinson 108.

18 Joinson 110.

GENERAL OLIVER OTIS HOWARD; Founder of Howard University

1   Oliver Otis Howard, *Autobiography of Oliver Otis Howard*, vol. 1 (New York: The Baker & Taylor Company, 1907) 7.

2   Howard 12-13.

3   Howard 14.

4   Howard 22.

5   John A. Carpenter, *Sword and Olive Branch* (New York: Fordham University Press, 1999) 7.

6   Howard 54.

7   Howard 73.

8   Howard 82.

9   Howard 81.

10 Howard 106.

11   Howard 108.

12   Howard 120-21.

13   Howard 124.

14   Howard 131.

15   Howard 132.

16   Howard 134.

17   Howard 249.

18   Howard 251.

19   Howard 324.

20   Howard 325.

21   Howard 326.

22   Howard 327.

23   Howard 348.

24   William B. Styple, *Generals in Bronze.*
      (Kearny, N.J.: Belle Grove Publishing Company, 2005) 180.

25   Howard 350-351.

26   Official Records, Series I, Vol. XXV, Part II, 554. (Later O.R., XXV, Part II, 554.)

27   Howard 363-64.

28   Howard 370-71.

29   Howard 374.

30   Howard 375.

31   Oliver Otis Howard, *Autobiography of Oliver Otis Howard*, vol. 2
      (New York: The Baker & Taylor Company, 1907) 211.

32   Styple 172.

33   Howard 207.

34   Howard 164.

35   Carpenter 235.

36   Howard 474-75.

37   Howard 545.

38   Howard 568-69.

39   Carpenter 299.

40   Howard 578.

BIBLIOGRAPHY

GENERAL DANIEL SIKLES; Colorful and Controversial

Brandt, Nat, *The Congressman Who Got Away with Murder*.
  Syracuse, N.Y: Syracuse University Press, 1991.

Conner, Jane Hollenbeck, *Lincoln in Stafford*. Fredericksburg, VA: Cardinal Press, 2006.

Haydon, F. Stansbury, *Military Ballooning during the Early Civil War*.
  Baltimore: The Johns Hopkins University Press, 1941.

Keneally, Thomas, *American Scoundrel: The Life of the Notorious Civil War General Dan Sickles*.
  New York: Nan A. Talese/Doubleday, 2002.

Salm-Salm, Princess Felix, *Ten Years of My Life*. New York: R. Worthington, 1877.

Clay-Clopton, Virginia, *A Belle of the Fifties: The Memoirs of Mrs. Clay of Alabama*.
  New York: Doubleday, Page & Company, 1904.

Styple, William B., Generals in Bronze; *Revealing Interviews with the Commanders of the Civil War*. Kearny, NJ: Belle Grove Publishing Co., 2005.

Swanberg, W.A., *Sickles the Incredible*. New York: Charles Scribner's Sons, 1956.

PRINCESS AGNES SALM-SALM; Righteous, Regal, or Relentless?

Barton, William E., *The Life of Clara Barton; Founder of the American Red Cross*. Vol. 2.
  New York: AMS Press, 1969.

Coffey, David, Soldier Princess; *The Life & Legend of Agnes Salm-Salm, in North America, 1861-1867*. College Station, Texas: Texas A&M University Press, 2002.

Malone, Dumas, Ed. *Dictionary of American Biography*, Vol. 8. New York: Charles Scribner's Sons, 1963.

Salm-Salm, Princess Felix, *Ten Years of My Life*. New York: R. Worthington, 1877.

Sandburg, Carl, *Abraham Lincoln; The War Years*. Vol. 2, New York: Harcourt, Brace & World, Inc, 1939.

CLARA BARTON; Angel of the Battlefield

Barton, William E., *The Life of Clara Barton; Founder of the American Red Cross*. 2 vols.
  New York: AMS Press, 1922.

Dictionary of American Biography, Vol. I, Allen Johnson, ed.
  New York: Charles Scribner's Sons, 1957.

Hamilton, Joseph, "Deeds of Heroism, Patriotism and Patience of Women in the Civil War and Spanish Wars," *Woman's Home Companion*, March, 1902.

Oates, Stephen B., *A Woman of Valor; Clara Barton and the Civil War*.
  New York: The Free Press, 1994.

Pryor, Elizabeth Brown, *Clara Barton; Official National Park Handbook*.
  Washington, D.C: Division of Publications, National Park Service, 1981.

Pryor, Elizabeth Brown, Clara Barton; *Professional Angel*.
  Philadelphia: University of Pennsylvania Press, (1987)1990.

Wolcott, Charles, History of the *Twenty-First Regiment, Massachusetts Volunteers*,
  Boston: Houghton, Mifflin & Co., 1892.

CLARA BARTON; Angel of the Battlefield

Conway, Moncure Daniel. Autobiography; Memories and Experiences of Moncure Daniel Conway. Vol. 1. Boston: Houghton, Mifflin and Company, 1904.

Glicksberg, Charles I. Walt Whitman and the Civil War. New York: A.S. Barnes and Company, Inc., 1963. (Originally pub. 1933 by University of Pennsylvania Press)

Loving, Jerome M., Ed. The Civil War Letters of George Washington Whitman. Durham, North Carolina: Duke State University Press, 1975.

Lowenfels, Walter, Ed. Walt Whitman's Civil War. New York: Da Capo Press, 1960.

Reynolds, David S. Walt Whitman's America: A Cultural Biography. New York: Alfred A. Knopf, Inc.,1995.

Roper, Robert. Now the Drum of War: Walt Whitman and his Brothers in the Civil War. New York: Walker & Company, 2008.

Ward, Candice, Ed. Walt Whitman; Civil War Poetry and Prose. Mineola, New York: Dover Publications, 1995.

WALT WHITMAN; The Good Gray Poet.

Conway, Moncure Daniel. Autobiography; Memories and Experiences of Moncure Daniel Conway. Vol. 1. Boston: Houghton, Mifflin and Company, 1904.

Glicksberg, Charles I. Walt Whitman and the Civil War. New York: A.S. Barnes and Company, Inc., 1963. (Originally pub. 1933 by University of Pennsylvania Press)

Loving, Jerome M., Ed. The Civil War Letters of George Washington Whitman. Durham, North Carolina: Duke State University Press, 1975.

Lowenfels, Walter, Ed. Walt Whitman's Civil War. New York: Da Capo Press, 1960.

Reynolds, David S. Walt Whitman's America: A Cultural Biography. New York: Alfred A. Knopf, Inc.,1995.

Roper, Robert. Now the Drum of War: Walt Whitman and his Brothers in the Civil War. New York: Walker & Company, 2008.

Ward, Candice, Ed. Walt Whitman; Civil War Poetry and Prose. Mineola, New York: Dover Publications, 1995.

DR. MARY EDWARDS WALKER; A Woman Doctor in Pants

Conway, Moncure Daniel. Autobiography; Memories and Experiences of Moncure Daniel Conway in Two Volumes. Vol. 2. Boston: Houghton, Mifflin and Company, 1904.

Graf, Mercedes. A Woman of Honor: Dr. Mary E. Walker and the Civil War. Gettysburg, PA: Thomas Publications, 2001.

Joinson, Carla. Civil War Doctor: The Story of Mary Walker. Greensboro, NC: Morgan Reynolds Publishing, 2007.

Joinson, Carla, "Mary Walker: A woman ahead of her time." Free Lance-Star, Town and County, Fredericksburg, VA, Nov. 18, 2006.

Leonard, Elizabeth D. Yankee Women; Gender Battles in the Civil War. New York: W.W. Norton & Company, 1994.

Mikaelian, Allen. Medal of Honor: Profiles of America's Military Heroes from the Civil War to the Present. New York: Hyperion, 2002.

Werlich, Robert. "Mary Walker: From Union Army Surgeon to Side Show Freak." Civil War Times Illustrated (1967), 46-49.

GENERAL OLIVER OTIS HOWARD; Founder of Howard University

Carpenter, John A. *Sword and Olive Branch; Oliver Otis Howard.*
New York: Fordham University Press, 1999.

Howard, Oliver Otis. *Autobiography of Oliver Otis Howard; Major General United States Army.*
2 Vols. New York: The Baker & Taylor Company, 1907.

Styple, William B. Ed. *Generals in Bronze; Interviewing the Commanders of the Civil War.*
Kearny, N.J.: Belle Grove Publishing Company, 2005.

ILLUSTRATION SOURCES

Most images used in this book were courtesy of the Library of Congress. Exceptions are followed with page numbers:

Dawson, William Forrest Ed., *Edwin Forbes Civil War Etchings.*
(New York: Dover Publications, Inc. 1985) 65

Findagrave.com 24

georcities.com 84

Harper's Weekly, June 11, 1864, 47

Harris, Tom, 6

HomeOfHeroes.com 83

National Library of Medicine, 75, 82

National Museum of Health and Medicine 8

National Park Service, Clara Barton, National Historic Site: 29, 32, 50, 52, 53

Salm-Salm, Princess Felix, *Ten Years of My Life.* (New York: R. Worthington, 1877) 22

Stackpole, Edward J., *Drama on the Rappahannock: The Fredericksburg Campaign.*
(Harrisburg: The Stackpole Co, 1957) 45

United States Army, 78

U.S. Army Military History Institute, Carlisle Barracks, PA Roger D. Hunt Collection 17

USPS and U.S. Department of Defense, DefenseLINK.com 86

West Point Library, U.S. Military Academy, West Point, NY Drawing by Durfee 43

White Oak Civil War Museum 7